THE COLLEGES OF CAMBRIDGE

THE COLLEGES OF OXFORD

BRYAN LITTLE

The
COLLEGES
of
CAMBRIDGE
1286-1973

Photographed by Edward Leigh

ARCO PUBLISHING COMPANY, INC.
New York

Published by Arco Publishing Company, Inc.
219 Park Avenue South, New York, N.Y. 10003

Copyright © 1973 by Bryan Little

Library of Congress Catalog Card Number 73-77337

ISBN 0-668-03301-0

Printed in Great Britain

CONTENTS

The Colleges exclusively or primarily for men are listed first, in the order of their foundation from Peterhouse to Churchill. Those which admit women undergraduates, now including Lucy Cavendish, are grouped together, while the graduate Colleges come at the end.

To the memory of

ARTHUR GRAY *and*
FREDERICK BRITTAIN

*Two members of my College who helped many towards
a wider knowledge of Cambridge.*

FOREWORD

SECTIONS of this book first appeared, from 1965 to 1970, as a series of articles in the *Cambridge Evening News*. I had taken care, not only to record the foundation and past history of each College, but in every one to discuss the changes and developments of the past few years.

The articles were very well received, and many readers, in Cambridge and elsewhere, strongly urged that this material should appear in book form. This book, with several important extra points to bring its record more fully up to date, is published in response to that demand.

While the articles were first being written, and during the times of their revision and updating, I had much kind help, and readily provided information on many aspects of the past history, and present life, of the Colleges in the University of Cambridge. I cannot list all those who aided me, but I must especially mention Professor Charles Wilson, of my own College, who suggested my name as a possible author of the articles to the *Cambridge News* (as it was then called), Mr Keith Whetstone who then edited the paper, and Mr Nicholas Herbert the present editor. But from 1965 till early in 1973 there has been no College in which senior members, all of them busy men or women, have not given me essential help; this has been specially valuable in respect of post-war activities.

B.D.G.L.
Bristol, 1973.

UNIVERSITY ORIGINS

NEITHER Cambridge nor Oxford started its career as a place of organised learning. Both of them were towns of some consequence for many decades before medieval scholars established within them the humble 'schools' which in time blossomed out into great Universities, and which brought about the gradual, somewhat piecemeal growth of the college system.

It is easy enough to see how it was that the *town* of Cambridge grew up where it did. What is much less obvious, in the 1970s when so much has happened to change the face of Cambridge, is the root-cause of the rise of this small town in the eastern counties to its great academic fame.

Like Oxford, Bridgwater, and many other towns, Cambridge started its career for the simple reason that here was a place where a navigable river could be easily reached, spanned by a bridge and still left usable by the commercial river-traffic that was of the utmost importance in the pre-railway age, and which survived long enough for Mrs Raverat to mention it, as a late Victorian phenomenon, in 'Period Piece'. A place where road and river traffic can readily meet is an obvious stopping-place for loading and unloading, for business talk, for warehouses, shops and inns.

Under the Romans the original Cambridge was a staging-point on a long military highway. The stiff rise of Castle Hill long made it a place of tactical importance. By the early Norman period the two settlements of Saxon Cambridge, one on each side of the river, had merged into one. It was as a commercial town, with a mainly military quarter on the river's left bank, that Cambridge seemed likely to find its future.

As in all such English towns there were several parish churches for the devotions of the inhabitants. Hospitals and other charitable foundations duly arose. But the bishop of the diocese, a powerful man and likely to

I

interfere in matters that displeased him, was far away at Lincoln, and then from 1109 some way down the river at Ely. Barnwell Priory, the one reasonably large monastic house, was eventually located well away to the east of the little commercial and market town. Ecclesiastically speaking, there was something of a vacuum in Cambridge. When this came to be filled, it was not by monks and canons regular, but by young scholars whose future career was mostly to be that of the secular clergy.

There were, of course, other towns to which they could equally well have gone. Some of them did, indeed, go for a short time to Northampton, as well as to Oxford whence many of them migrated to what some might have thought an unpromising site among the low eminences and dank river fogs of the Granta basin. Yet Cambridge, a county town, a market town, and a river port on the eastern side of England, had certain advantages which made it much better, as the site of a great seat of learning, than some might have thought in those opening years of the thirteenth century. Some of these were connected with the disposition, around 1200, of England's centres of civil and ecclesiastical power. A more decisive reason, perhaps, was purely geographical.

The king, in those days of hot-tempered, overbearing Plantagenet sovereigns, was not always the best of neighbours to churchmen and scholars. In the year 1209, when some discontented Oxonians are known to have migrated to Cambridge, King John was on the throne and Becket's death was still fresh in the memories of Englishmen. Though the king, and the government machine, moved more than they do today there was a growing tendency for Westminster to become the country's capital. London and its immediate area could well prove an awkward place for academic habitation should disputes break out between the University and the Crown.

Medieval bishops could also be uneasy neighbours for academic communities, so that there was something to be said for not having a fledgling University in a cathedral city. Colleges like Peterhouse and Jesus at Cambridge and Lincoln and Brasenose at Oxford indeed proved that England's ancient Universities could be kindly favoured by their diocesan bishops. But distance, on the whole, tended to lend enchantment to bishops as seen from the schools. So Oxford, all through the Middle Ages, happily remained almost as far as it could from its bishop at Lincoln. For Cambridge, the more modest distance of Ely would have been reasonable enough in the transport conditions of those times.

A still greater convenience, when one remembers the population distribution and the transport situation of Plantagenet England was the precise location of Cambridge between *two* zones of heavy population and not in the midst of only one.

Two vital points about the geography of early Cambridge were these: it was not *in* the Fens but at the extreme upper or southern end of that long wedge of marshy, somewhat trackless country. While the Fenland waterways were to be of great value for the freightage to Cambridge of heavy building-materials they do not seem to have been much used as a passenger highway. A man wishing to travel from, say central Norfolk to Northamptonshire, would find it more convenient to go southwards to Cambridge, cross the river, and then strike north and west towards the eastern Midlands. But if Cambridge, unlike Ely, was not a truly Fenland town neither was it thoroughly embedded in East Anglia. In Saxon times its river had formed part of the border between Mercia on the Granta's left bank and East Anglia on the other side. Reckoned in modern terms the twin settlement of pre-Conquest Cambridge stood poised, between the eastern Midlands and the eastern counties, on a vital point of communication between the two.

Medieval Cambridge was thus so sited that it could draw traders, travellers and scholars from two regions which were both of them more populous and prosperous, in comparison with the rest of England, than they are today. London, with its population large by the standards of those times, was not too far away to the south. The 'business end' of Yorkshire, in those days the district close to York itself, the wool-growing uplands of the Yorkshire Wolds, and the Humberside district of Beverley and Hull, was easy to reach through the counties of the eastern Midlands. So Cambridge was very well placed to blossom forth as a University of national standing, drawing scholars from populous East Anglia, from the eastern Midlands and the north as readily as Oxford was to attract students from the West of England and Wales.

So one sees, on a reckoning of geography and of the social layout of thirteenth-century England, that the flight of scholars from Oxford to Cambridge may not have been a wholly haphazard affair. But once the scholars got established in Cambridge, and once their numbers increased with new arrivals from areas which were more accessible from the Granta than from the Isis, some difficulties arose.

Lecture rooms, or 'schools', for the Masters were not unduly hard to provide. Many of the earliest lectures must in any case have been given in the halls of fair-sized private houses. But living accommodation, alike for lecturers and their hearers, was a more difficult matter. Then as now, undergraduate lodging was a social and financial problem. So we find, in

1231, that the King complained of extortionate lodgings for scholars in both Oxford and Cambridge. He feared that the students, particularly those from abroad whose presence in 'Oxbridge' brought prestige to England, would leave the country in disgust. He gave orders that two University Masters and two respected townsmen should fix the rents which the scholars were to pay.

Yet it seems that these well-meaning measures were of no lasting avail. The rise of the Colleges was eventually, and to within the past few years, the solution to the housing of Cambridge's growing academic population.

THE NEED FOR COLLEGES

WE have long been accustomed to think of Oxford and Cambridge Colleges as complex yet complete unities, containing within themselves—and on a reasonably lavish scale—all the elements one associates with a medieval Christian seat of learning. Only within the last century, and in particular during very recent years, has it been conceivable for a College in either of the ancient Universities to be without its chapel. But for the most part no College has seemed truly itself without a chapel as well as a hall. Libraries, common rooms, and offices now seem as essential as the living and working rooms of those who teach and those who learn.

Yet this is not how the Colleges of Oxford and Cambridge started. Their growth took place in a typically English, haphazard way, and it was only slowly that they came to contain what one now takes as a matter of course. In their earliest days they had little of the neat, systematic planning of the contemporary monasteries; it was about a century after the endowed colleges had first been started before a complete, tautly co-ordinated College was planned by its founder for erection at Oxford, and for building in a single operation.

Nor were the colleges the first expedient tried out in medieval Oxford and Cambridge to cope with the severe difficulties of student lodging.

In the early days of the old Universities, and indeed for some centuries after their foundation, the students were nearly all of them younger than those of today. They were unversed in the ways of the world, and many were extremely poor. They were ill-equipped to deal on their own with the rough-and-tumble of medieval town life. They were often exploited by the keepers of their lodgings, and disputes over money were but one of the causes which led to brawls, riots, fights with townsmen, and sometimes to serious bloodshed. In the pre-collegiate days at Oxford and Cambridge the lodging problem caused chaos and unhappiness and cried out for some remedy; the same difficulties are not unknown nowadays both at 'Oxbridge' and in the towns which house non-collegiate Universities.

The first solution (and as it proved no more than a partial one) was that now employed to house some students attending the 'red-brick' Universities. At Oxford and Cambridge the University as such did not concern itself (as a modern University is bound to do) with the ownership of hostels and halls of residence. The provision of such lodging-places was left to private persons, and although those who did provide them were senior members of the University, and were approved for this purpose by the academic authorities, the buildings themselves did not belong to the University.

So the situation was not unlike that which one finds with some hostels for students, in cities like Bristol which contain growing Universities, where religious denominations and other bodies will sometimes provide hostels for students who are strangers to England and may sometimes find ordinary lodging hard to obtain.

The medieval halls and hostels of Oxford and Cambridge were smaller, less sophisticated buildings than those now erected under private auspices as student hostels, and they did not have to face such modern complications as planning permission and building by-laws. But the principle was the same in the thirteenth century as it is nowadays for these 'unofficial' buildings for the accommodation of students away from the hazards and difficulties of purely private 'digs'.

The academic halls and hostels of medieval Oxford and Cambridge existed before the colleges. For some centuries they and the colleges flourished side by side; it was long before the students who were under-graduate members of colleges exceeded the number of those who found their accommodation in the halls and hostels.

Where these halls and hostels differed from ordinary lodgings was not so much in their structure, for many of them were no more than rented private houses, but in their day-to-day control. For their landlord-tenant relationship was not between young, somewhat bewildered students and hostile townsmen, but between students and the dons of early days. The Masters, or teachers, were not always the owners of these early lodging places, but as the tenants of the townsmen who owned the buildings they were the people to whom the student lodger looked. Quarrels and difficulties there may well have been, but a student who had lodgings in such an establishment was likely to find more sympathy than he would get from some poorly educated citizen.

So we find, in both Oxford and Cambridge, that many of these halls and hostels came into being. Some were never more than simple town dwellings. But a few, like Hart Hall, Broadgates Hall, and St Edmund Hall at Oxford, were of a recognisably 'collegiate' type; these three halls were all of them the nuclei of eventual colleges. Structurally similar, so one gathers, was St Bernard's Hostel at Cambridge, of which Andrew Doket was Principal before he founded Queens' College. The halls of these places were like those of small manor houses, and although they lacked formally licensed chapels they could contain private oratories for the prayers of their inmates.

Some of the larger halls reached such a degree of stability that they got informally associated with colleges; they became, as it were, most useful 'annexes' on which those colleges could rely for extra student-accommodation. In some cases the colleges actually came to be the owners of what had once been private hostels.

Yet although some of these halls and hostels found it possible to last for some centuries, with no pressing financial worries provided that there were always inmates to pay their rents, they had some serious disadvantages. As those who lived in them had to pay rents out of their own pockets they were of limited use to the poorest of those who wished to attend the schools. As they were unendowed they had no safe guarantee either of permanent existence or of any ability to give financial help to the students who dwelt in them.

Although several of them did in fact last all through the Middle Ages, and then only faded away because of the colleges' increasing practice of taking 'pensioners' or paying-students, the death of a Master of Arts in charge of a hostel, or some change of mind on the part of a townsman who owned such a building, might bring about its closure. Only the regular endowment of an academic institution, and its total independence of such hazards, could assure its physical continuance and the permanence of its good work.

The early colleges of Oxford and Cambridge were therefore brought into being by the shortcomings of the private lodging and semi-private hostels which existed before them. The essence of a college, as of a monastery or an almshouse, was its stable financial endowment. Residential buildings, on a more or less regular plan, soon followed. But they were not, at first, indispensable for an endowed foundation. The early history of University College, Oxford, well illustrates this point.

William of Durham, the priest who left money for a foundation to support about a dozen needy Masters of Arts, died in 1249. The University, to which he left a considerable sum for the execution of his plan, bought three houses whose rents would aid these graduates in the pursuit of their higher studies. It was as if, in our own time and for the same purpose, a similar sum was invested in the stock of, let us say I.C.I., Lever Brothers, and British Leyland.

It was not for some 30 years that the little society had a home in any particular Oxford premises, and the present site of Oxford's oldest endowed foundation was not bought till the 1330s. The earliest buildings of this college were very small. As time went on, and as the buildings grew in size, 'University' College became self-governing and wholly separate from the central academic authority whence it took its name.

An important point about these early days was that the first colleges were not originally meant for the housing of undergraduates, but for a group of men who were thought to stand in even greater need of financial security and residential peace and quiet. The first inmates of the early colleges were all of them graduates. Some were lecturers and teachers, others pursued higher studies—the medieval equivalents of the post-graduate research workers who are so numerous in Oxford and Cambridge today.

These early colleges were as All Souls' at Oxford has constantly remained, while to mention a modern Cambridge parallel the situation was as if Corpus Christi College solely consisted nowadays of Leckhampton House across the Backs.

We shall see, in later chapters, how some of these early colleges were at first like Fitzwilliam House in more modern times, being no more than converted dwelling-houses. Even when they started to expand, their growth was sometimes slow and haphazard. Only rarely was there any initial attempt at complete or systematic collegiate planning, or at any building process like that which tended to follow the foundation of a new Cistercian monastery.

Many Masters of Arts and graduate students of those early days by no means required the endowed accommodation provided by the colleges. In any case those little colleges could house only a small proportion of the senior academics in residence. Here again one senses a very modern parallel, for we have found that the highly developed collegiate system of the 1960s could not absorb the vastly greater number and variety of the graduates of many universities who came to research and teach in Cambridge.

But in the fourteenth century the authorities of Cambridge's first colleges found that organised places of learning needed specially built halls and other buildings of some size and sophistication if they were to perform the tasks appointed for them by their founders. We must turn to the story, one by one, of each college to see how in varying ways reality was given in clunch, mortar and freestone, and eventually in brick and concrete, to these more mature ideas for the physical reality of a college.

PETERHOUSE. Old Court: the Chapel and its Loggia

KING'S HALL. King's Hostel, looking East

PETERHOUSE

THE distinctive, irremovable glory of Peterhouse is that it is the oldest by foundation of all Cambridge colleges. In its buildings, only a single doorway and some walling remain as clear evidence for Peterhouse's existence before 1300. But the fascinating, somewhat complex facts of its early history are well known, and one can be sure that this southerly Cambridge college, small in numbers but rich in history, has now been at work, on its present site, for nearly seven centuries.

Yet the early story of this first collegiate foundation in Cambridge was not wholly simple or straightforward, and had its founder's plans gone as he first intended, neither the site nor the name of the college would have been the same as they are today. Although Peterhouse's foundation date is given as 1284, the college's story really starts in the year 1280, and looks back to a still earlier date in English academic history. For it was in 1280 that Hugh Balsham, the Benedictine monk who was Bishop of Ely from 1257 to 1286, took steps to improve the supply not of graduate monks but of academically educated secular clergy. He obtained a licence to place non-monastic scholars into the existing hospital, or almshouse, of St John the Evangelist.

This charitable institution, whose poor inmates were not, by this new scheme to house scholars and almsmen in the same precincts, to be defrauded of their benefits, stood on the site of St John's College. It had been founded in the twelfth century, and a fine piscina survives from its chapel which was built about 1200. Some of its endowments were to be reserved for the maintenance of the bishop's scholars, and he must have hoped that his arrangements would be lasting. One may also assume that had this first expedient of Bishop Balsham been a permanent success St John's College might never have been founded, or that at all events the second of Cambridge's Beaufort colleges would have been started elsewhere and would have had some other dedication.

What is also of interest, when we look at these earliest days of the Cambridge colleges, is the rule of life laid down for these first inmates of an endowed academic foundation in the younger of our two ancient Universities. In this same connection we also come across a historic situation which might have meant that Oxford had one college less and Cambridge one more.

Walter de Merton, Chancellor of England and later the Bishop of Rochester, was like Bishop Balsham in his desire to see a better educated body of secular clergy. In 1262 he made arrangements for the Augustinian Priory of Merton in Surrey to support some scholars studying at a University (not necessarily that of Oxford). Two years later he enlarged his foundation, giving it headquarters neither at Oxford nor Cambridge but at Malden, not far from Merton. There was still no geographical limitation on the place where his beneficiaries should pursue their studies, for Walter de Merton laid it down that his scholars could go to Oxford, 'or elsewhere where a *Studium* happens to flourish'.

Then in 1270 he bought property for the eventual siting of a college, away from Surrey, at both Oxford and Cambridge. There were various political factors which made it possible that a new foundation at Oxford would be somewhat precarious, so Walter de Merton seems to have shrewdly provided for a foundation in whichever of the two University towns proved more convenient. His Cambridge purchase comprised various lands and the 'Stone House', the late Norman domestic building later known as 'The School of Pythagoras' and now, in its restored condition, part of St John's College. But in 1274 he plumped finally for Oxford, moving his scholars to Merton College there and giving them definitive new statutes which could serve as a model for other founders of like mind. In that same year he became Bishop of Rochester, and in another three years he died of drowning. Merton College, Cambridge, never became a reality. But the rules of de Merton's Oxford College, in its early days the largest of the senior University's endowed foundations, formed the pattern chosen for his own pioneering venture in Cambridge by Bishop Balsham who was, for three years, Bishop Merton's episcopal colleague and perhaps his friend and confidant.

One may also trace an architectural parallel between Merton's Oxford college and its opposite number in Cambridge. For it became clear, while the old chapel of St John's College was being pulled down in the 1860s, that this fabric which seemed to date from the early Tudor period was really a splendid, much re-windowed rectangular choir in the 'geometrical' style of Gothic that was in vogue about 1280. What seems likely is that when Bishop Balsham introduced his scholars into St John's Hospital he at once started a noble chapel for the joint use of his academics and the almsmen already on the premises. This building, whose windows partly survived till the mid-Victorian demolition, could have been a precedent, not only for Little St Mary's church which eventually served Balsham's scholars on their second site, but also for the early Decorated choir soon started for the members of Merton College at Oxford.

The brethren and almsmen of St John's Hospital and Bishop Balsham's scholars soon found that they could not harmoniously share the same premises. The Bishop (unlike Bishop Fisher in another 227 years) must have felt that he could not well suppress or transfer the long-established hospital. He had no alternative, while time sufficed, but to move his scholars. He had been Bishop of Ely since 1257 and he must, by 1284 when he made the move, have been an elderly man by the standards of those times, and unsure of long continuance in this life. As it happened he died in another two years, having had no time, while still alive, to endow his scholars as amply as those of Bishop Walter de Merton. What was done, 1284–85, was to carry out the physical move, and to obtain a Royal Charter which sanctioned the transfer of the scholars to two houses, or hostels. These stood on a site just west of the Trumpington road, not far outside the southern, or Trumpington, gate of Cambridge. They stood close to one of Cambridge's two churches dedicated to St Peter. It is from this move, and not from Bishop Balsham's original foundation, that the name of Peterhouse, or St Peter's College, derived.

The first buildings, as in some others among the earliest Cambridge colleges, were no more than ordinary dwelling houses, with others like them on each side of these houses and their long, narrow gardens running down towards the river and Coe Fen. What first made Peterhouse, as it did the other Colleges in their foundation days, was not the character of its building but the fixed nature of its financial endowment. Arrangements were now made for the redistribution of the hospital's property between the brethren and almsmen who stayed on in the old site, and the Bishop's scholars in their new abode outside Trumpington Gate. As Bishop Balsham lay dying in 1286 he did something to make up for the modesty of his College's revenues. He gave Peterhouse 300 marks (£200), in those days a most generous benefaction. With this money a strip of extra land was bought to the south of the two existing houses, which the scholars must by now have felt to be too cramped for their needs. Their first move, now that they had this addition to their site, was to build, by 1290, a new and beautiful hall (*aulam perpulchram*) which could answer, in late thirteenth-century Cambridge, to the hall, with its undercroft and transomed windows, which served Merton College at Oxford.

This hall, much rebuilt and altered, survives as the present hall of Peterhouse. It is a strange coincidence that the southern doorway of its screens passage much resembles the simple doorway which remains in the even more drastically Victorianised hall at Merton. What was also important was that here in Peterhouse, as in other early Cambridge colleges, the first communal structure built in the college was not the chapel but the hall which could serve alike for eating, tuition, and for other gatherings of those on the foundation. These early days of Peterhouse are significant for the evolution of more colleges than this oldest one in Cambridge.

Not long after the building of its hall, Peterhouse added greatly to its site. The way in which it did so foreshadowed the method by which several later Cambridge colleges obtained or increased their territory. When Bishop Balsham moved his scholars from the Hospital of St John to the nucleus of Peterhouse, some ground immediately to the south of the college was still occupied by the stone house, chapel, and other buildings of the Friars of the Penance of Jesus, known from the rough austerity of their habit as the Friars of the Sack.

Their Order, like some other small bodies of friars, was not allowed to continue till the end of the Middle Ages. Their establishments slowly dwindled to extinction, and in 1307 their Cambridge property was bought by Peterhouse. The ground was not used for buildings, but provided space for the enclosed deer-park which was among the college's most charming features. More important still, its purchase looked forward to the way in which the land of the religious houses of Cambridge from time to time provided ground, or materials, for the building up of a number of colleges far increased beyond the single one which existed in the Cambridge of the year 1300.

For two centuries after its territorial expansion in 1307 the history of Peterhouse was that of a small college, not very wealthy and no more than moderately distinguished. Late in the fourteenth century the future Cardinal Beaufort was there; his presence in Peterhouse fits, if it does not explain, a Lancastrian trend in the college's later sympathies. The hall, and Bishop Balsham's two houses, seem, for some 150 years, to have satisfied its accommodation needs. More significant, in the very middle of the fourteenth century, was the building of Little St Mary's to replace the dilapidated Norman fabric of St Peter's church. The new building was dedicated in 1352, and is particularly beautiful work in the Decorated style. Though its status was always that of a parish church it was also used, for regular worship and burial, by the members of Peterhouse, and the college was and is the patron of the living. An upstairs gallery was later built to make a physical link between the college and its parish church, and the whole design of this attractive building is more that of a college chapel than that which one associates with an ordinary parish church.

It was not until about 1430 that anything more was done to carry on with Peterhouse's buildings. By the end of the fifteenth century the north, south and west ranges of the front court had been finished. They included sets of rooms and a library. Their construction, as we can see and as we find it documented in Peterhouse's excellent building records, was mainly in clunch. This was quarried at Cherry Hinton, and some brick was also used in the northern range which lies closest to Little St Mary's.

Early in the sixteenth century, Peterhouse had an important Master in Henry Hornby. He seems, from his connections, to have been aligned with the liberalising Roman Catholics. For he had been an official in the household of the Lady Margaret Beaufort. He was one of her executors, and had links with Colet, Erasmus, and Sir Thomas More. The numbers of those in the college now increased, and some leading positions in the University came to be held by Peterhouse men. In the stirring decades of the Reformation, life in the college seems to have been comparatively placid. Some Peterhouse men were among the Reformers, while others were more inclined to the continuance of the older religious ways. Among these latter was Dr Andrew Perne, the college's Master for over 30 years until his death in 1589. Though he had been appointed under Mary I he seems, more than his contemporary, the famous Master of Caius, to have accommodated his opinions to political conditions. Numbers at Peterhouse rose steeply in his time, for although in 1572 there were some 70 to 80 men plus a few 'poor scholars' on the college books, in another nine years the inmates of Peterhouse had increased to 154—by far the highest figure up to that date and not many below the college's modest membership in more modern times.

As in many Cambridge colleges, the first half of the seventeenth century was a stirring period for Peterhouse. Despite its varied religious inclinations under the Tudors it was now solidly ranged on the Laudian, High Church, Royalist side of the great struggle of those times. This phase in Peterhouse's history had started in James I's reign, in the Mastership of Leonard Mawe.

The same tendencies were even stronger under Matthew Wren, the uncle of Sir Christopher Wren the architect, who was a Pembroke man and later Bishop of Ely. It was Matthew Wren who started the Laudian Gothic chapel (Cambridge's chief equivalent to the 'survivalist' Gothic of Stuart Oxford and similar to the chapel of Lincoln College, Oxford) whose fanciful façade partly closes the eastern side of the college's front court. Its consecration in 1632 was a major demonstration of Laudian ritualism, and in later years the ornaments and ceremonies under Dr Cosin, Wren's successor and later the Bishop of Durham, included such controversial items as bowing to the altar, a crucifix and lighted candles, and the burning of incense. The chapel at Peterhouse not unnaturally became especially obnoxious to the Puritans, and when at the time of the Civil War, with its Parliamentary control of the eastern counties, William Dowsing paid his anti-ritualist visit to Peterhouse he was as gleeful in his destruction of the chapel's new Laudian adornments as he was, all over East Anglia, in the smashing of medieval images and glass.

Another aspect of Cosin's connection with Peterhouse was the revival of the college's old connection with the North, in particular with Northumberland and Durham which lay in Cosin's diocese. For many years, and well into the eighteenth century, Peterhouse was a favoured college for the sons of good families in those counties, and also from the North Riding of Yorkshire.

In Peterhouse, as in some other Cambridge colleges, the eighteenth century was a somewhat slack and placid period, with a continuing tradition of legal studies in this particular college. It now contained some wealthy and idle fellow commoners as well as the fee-paying pensioners who had long been well established among its members. Two of these fellow commoners were the men responsible for the unkind practical joke, playing on the poet Thomas Gray's great fear of fire, which in 1756 caused Gray to move from Peterhouse, across Trumpington Street, to more congenial company at Pembroke. The Fellows' Building, where this episode occurred, was fairly new at that time, being Peterhouse's Palladian addition to its much older buildings. Its first court, like some other clunch-built ranges in Cambridge was ashlared and Palladianised, on its inner side, about the time of Gray's migration. But plans for another new building, to lie south of the chapel, were never carried out. So Peterhouse's street frontage was left as an outstandingly attractive sequence of Carolean brickwork, survivalist Gothic, and Palladian classical.

The last years of the eighteenth century saw Peterhouse under the longest of its Masterships, that of Francis Barnes who held office from 1788 to 1838; though he lived to see Queen Victoria on the throne he was the last man in Cambridge to wear the wig which had been fashionable in mid-Georgian times. He is said, from the time of his election, to have been wholly unsuited for his post, and he was certainly an unchanging figure of the old school. But he may have been underrated, for the college was financially prosperous in his time, and its buildings were well maintained. Barnes's portrait, perhaps a caricature, shows him with a toothless, big-nosed profile like that of 'Mr Punch'. It was in Barnes's Mastership that the Rev. Francis Gisborne, a former Fellow of Peterhouse and a man of great wealth, in 1817 made the large benefaction which caused the erection, to the west of the medieval buildings, of the early Gothic revivalist Gisborne Court. But by the time of Barnes's death Peterhouse's numbers were falling, and in 1842 the college's undergraduates numbered only 39.

The Victorian period was one of steady renewal for Peterhouse. Mathematics became an important subject in the college, and among many able Scotsmen who went to Peterhouse the most eminent was Lord Kelvin, who came up as an undergraduate in the 1840s and who, as Sir William Thomson, became a Fellow in 1872. It was Lord Kelvin who in 1884 marked Peterhouse's 600th anniversary by arranging for the installation in the college of electric light, at a time when that novelty had yet to illuminate any other buildings in the University.

A few years later came the commencement of a new Peterhouse tradition, for in 1894 history was added to its scholarship subjects. From then onwards, with such prominent names as A. W. Ward, H. W. V. Temperley, Professor David Knowles, and H. C. Butterfield, historical studies in this oldest of all Cambridge colleges have been notably strong. Another feature of Peterhouse, lasting to our own time when its undergraduate numbers are kept at about 200, is its deliberately, and happily, modest size. Nor is it the college's policy to admit undergraduates to read subjects in which it has no teaching Fellows. Another, more domestic feature of life in Peterhouse in this present century was the excellence, in the years just before the late war, of the college's cuisine. I myself, though not a Peterhouse man, have personal memories of the culinary feats achieved under that outstanding chef, the late Mr Cooper.

Our final passage in this chapter concerns a recent Peterhouse benefaction, and its important visible results.

The late Mr William Stone was a Peterhouse man who died, a few years ago, at the age of 101. From his property interests in The Albany and elsewhere in the West End of London he was known as 'The Squire of Piccadilly'. He was a millionaire at the time of his death, and it was then found that he had left to his old college the residue of his large estate.

The money has been laid out on the endowment of Research Fellowships and on the building, not far from the Peterhouse property of St Peter's Terrace which has in part been fitted out as rooms 'in college', of the William Stone Building. Its site is at the southern end of the territory of English Croft which Peterhouse bought in the reign of Elizabeth I; a large part of it was sold in 1823 to become the site of the Fitzwilliam Museum.

The William Stone Building, by Professor Sir Leslie Martin, is a revolutionary departure among the domestic buildings of a Cambridge college. For it is an eight-storey tower-block of flats, for eight unmarried Fellows and 24 undergraduates, in splendidly shaped and detailed yellow brick. It has the living-rooms on its floors set back in succession so that each room gets the maximum of sunlight and a good southern aspect. This new Peterhouse block is certainly among the best contemporary buildings in Cambridge, and is in my opinion a more sympathetic work than the same architect's new court for Caius. In its background of generous benefaction it stands well in succession to Peterhouse's earlier gifts from Francis Gisborne (who was also a generous benefactor to the naval charity of Greenwich Hospital) and Bishop Balsham.

KING'S HALL

By the year 1290 the small college of Peterhouse was reasonably set on its long career. The collegiate system, though now inaugurated in Cambridge, was as yet a small element in the life of the *Studium Generale* established in the eastern counties. When in another 30 years we come again to the process of college-founding we have to see it, as Dr Cobban of Trinity College has shown, as part of a major development, in the political and administrative policy of the Crown, which much affected the whole position and national standing of Cambridge University.

By 1317 the reign of Edward II had run half of its turbulent course. The king, who had never forgiven the murder of his beloved favourite, Piers Gaveston, was in sharp conflict with powerful aristocrats whose craving for power and moral susceptibilities had been frustrated and ruffled by Edward's relationship with Gaveston. As the Lords Ordainer improved their position, the King withdrew into the reliable fastness of his royal household. He hoped that his careful filling of its appointments would keep him some of the power he had lost.

Educated men for these civil service posts could, in those days, come only from the ordained ranks of the Church, non-resident clergy being financed, while performing government work, by the benefices and other Church preferments which they held *in absentia*. These men could best serve the royal purpose if they were caught young, from such circles as the clerks and the choristers of the Chapel Royal, and then sent for further intellectual training to one of England's two available Universities.

Dr Cobban has established that the one at Oxford then stood somewhat low in royal esteem. For back in 1312 the clerks of the University and the burgesses of the town had been asked for help and advice over the fate of

Gaveston who had been arrested by his political enemies. They had declined
to be concerned. Though their indifference was but one factor in Gaveston's
inevitable fate they could, by their mere inaction, have incurred Edward's
hostility. Dr Cobban has further pointed out that Edward II was also at odds
with Oxford over the position in that University of his favourite friars, the
Dominicans. He would thus be disposed to turn a kind eye on the smaller,
but none the less well-established place of higher education in the eastern
counties.

Cambridge may thus have seemed a better training place for the clerics
who would help to man his administrative machine. Two subsequent events
can be linked together as strong pointers in the same direction. One was the
placing in Cambridge of a royally founded society. The other was the
procurement for the University of a Bull from Pope John XXII. Dr Cobban's
research has revealed that this did not, as was formerly believed, presume
to confer the status of a *Studium Generale* on Cambridge University, but
that the Bull amounted to official papal confirmation of an already existing
status.

The foundation of King's Hall was in 1317, and the Papal *roboratio* (not
fundatio) of the *Studium Generale* came in the following year. But the
preliminary proceedings were simultaneous, and the two episodes are
two aspects of a policy trend which gave a strong boost to the academic
fortunes of Cambridge.

For the first twenty years the young scholars of Edward II's Cambridge
foundation lived in a rented house. The money for their maintenance came
from the royal revenues, and the King gave them some books in 1321. Then
in 1337, King Edward III arranged for the more durable settlement of this
organisation for the Cambridge training of clerks and Court officials.
He formally established King's Hall as a lasting element in the University.
He also bought them a large house as a permanent home. This house, shaped
as a three-sided court, faced the lane, from High (now Trinity) Street
down towards the river, which was soon, from the royal college itself,
named King's Childer Lane. Its position determined the basic plan of
a college whose site was soon enlarged. Some regular endowments were
also given to the college, increasing its resources beyond the sums available
from the royal coffers.

The college had a warden and 32 scholars. Those who came there to
study at Cambridge were many of them relations of officials at Court,
themselves being destined for similar posts. One may almost think of King's
Hall as a medieval version of a staff college for administrators.

The Hundred Years' War and the Black Death brought trouble to this royal college. But its largely official character continued, and about 1375 its systematic, though somewhat unambitious rebuilding was started. A small four-sided court was slowly built. It did not reach as far south as King's Childer Lane and did not occupy all of the college's reasonably spacious site. This was partly because King's Hall had still to use the house bought in 1337, the new buildings not being complete and fully occupied till about 1438.

By this time the college had finished its fine Gate Tower leading out to King's Childer Lane, this being the 'Edward III' tower later moved backwards against the western end of Trinity chapel. Another building surviving from this slow process of construction is the simple, homely range which was once the western range of King's Hall's enclosed court. One finds it, past the present location of the 'Edward III' tower, in King's Hostel whose back looks out towards the river over Trinity's secluded bowling green.

By the middle of the 1440s King Henry VI was heavily committed to his rich foundations of Eton and King's. So strong was the new current of royal favour that in 1447–48 the two new colleges were empowered not only to appoint the inmates of King's Hall, but also to make it new statutes. Their control of King's Hall lasted for some years. But the Wars of the Roses, and the political fall of Henry VI, restored the fortunes of the older college. In 1462 the Yorkist King Edward IV gave it back its old status.

The relations of high officials were still among its scholars, and a few pensioners, or fee-paying students, were still in residence. A fair-sized chapel was started about 1464, and when this was finished King's Hall gave up its regular use of All Saints' church which then stood on its old site just East of Trinity Street. It was on this eastern side of the college that the finest and most famous of additions was made to the buildings of King's Hall. For the splendid gate tower which is now the Great Gate of Trinity was built between 1518 and 1535. Its heraldry, with references to Edward III and his sons, still reminds us that the great college now entered by this gate was not the first one in this part of academic Cambridge.

For the first 60 years of the Tudor régime the life of King's Hall seems to have continued on the normal lines. The college was richer than most others in Cambridge, and its records prove the variety and value of its possessions. Late in Henry VIII's reign its fortunes were wholly changed; the events which included its extinction were the last acts in a crisis which could have overwhelmed the University itself. For an Act of Parliament of 1544 had empowered the King to dissolve any college in Oxford or Cambridge. It seemed that this Act might be enforced. But the university authorities appealed to Queen Catherine Parr. She appears to have persuaded her ailing husband not to grant any demands for dissolution that might come from courtiers who were anxious to lay their hands on college revenues. Instead, the King decided to give substance to the old idea that he might found a splendid Cambridge college which would rival or surpass Christ Church at Oxford.

King's Hall, with its royal antecedents (particularly with Edward III whom the early Tudor monarchs went out of their way to honour as an ancestor) and its financial links with the Crown, was an obvious nucleus for such a foundation. It could also provide much of the new college's site. So, in 1546, King's Hall ceased to exist. But Trinity, which succeeded it and Michaelhouse, is not without buildings which once belonged to the more important of the two colleges which now made way for the mammoth among Cambridge's royal foundations. It has also left some splendid original records; these include accounts which make up the longest single series of paper documents left by any college in Britain.

For the compilation of this chapter I had much kind help from Dr A. B. Cobban, of Trinity College, who has written a full-scale book on the history of King's Hall. He has dealt with the question of the Bull of 1318 in the article entitled 'Edward II, Pope John XXII, and the University of Cambridge' in the 'Bulletin of the John Rylands Library', Vol. 47, No. I September 1964.

MICHAELHOUSE

SEVEN years after Edward II sent his young students of the Chapel Royal to study at Cambridge the small College of Michaelhouse was founded there by a prominent priest in the royal service who stood out as a leading adherent of the king. This act in the year 1324 can be seen as a part of the same deliberate Court policy which favoured Cambridge above Oxford, and which meant that in the first half of the fourteenth century seven Colleges were founded in Cambridge against three in England's other University town.

Far less can now be seen of Michaelhouse than of King's Hall. That does not, however, mean that the eventual second component of Trinity was any the less an academic reality.

The founder of Michaelhouse was Hervey de Stanton, a priest-cum-lawyer from Suffolk who held numerous prebendal livings, had some judicial posts, and was also employed in high offices of State. He was a friend of Bishop Stapledon of Exeter, another close adherent of Edward II who had, in 1314, founded Exeter College, Oxford. As a strong supporter of the king he was Chancellor of the Exchequer from 1316 till Edward's political fall in 1326. It may interest the present Master of Trinity to recall that the founder of one of his College's component elements was a predecessor in one of the many political offices which he himself has held. Michaelhouse also has the distinction of being one of the only two Cambridge Colleges to have had, as one of its heads, a canonised saint.

De Stanton's plans for Michaelhouse went back at least as early as 1323, for in that year he bought a house, and with it the gift of the living St Michael's church. The house stood opposite the church, on a site now occupied by Tree Court of Caius College. Had they actually lived there the priests of de Stanton's foundation would have been closer than they actually were to the church which de Stanton rebuilt for the joint use of the College and the parish.

But in 1324 the wealthy founder bought another large house, to the West of this further purchase and facing what was then called St Michael's Lane and is now the gloomy thoroughfare of Trinity Lane. This house, with another next door, became the first home of the new College. Michael-house's site, later enlarged, covered the south-western part of what is now the Great Court of Trinity. Other additions to the property included several private hostels. Some of these, like St Gregory's and Angel Hostels, covered ground later absorbed into the expanse of Trinity's Great Court. As the late Professor Trevelyan pointed out in his short history of Trinity College the 'future spaciousness of Trinity' was determined by the piece-meal purchases of ground by the authorities of Michaelhouse and King's Hall.

Michaelhouse was not a large College, and as it disappeared in 1546 it never received the pensioners, or fee-paying students, who in time became a growing element elsewhere. Its first members were a Master, three Masters of Arts who were in priest's orders, and two bachelors of arts who had the same ecclesiastical status. All of these were to be on higher studies in philosophy and theology, as also was a subdeacon who belonged to the College. Later endowments slightly increased the number of Michael-house's Fellows, and some 'poor scholars' were also added to the College's endowed inmates. But its fellowships never exceeded seventeen, and for so small a body the little College was well enough endowed for its inhabitants to live in comfort, and for its later buildings to be on a fairly ambitious scale.

The most important original relic of Michaelhouse is St Michael's church as rebuilt by Hervey de Stanton. It reminds us, as do St Edward's and St Benet's, that some churches long had a dual function as College chapels, and as the normal worshipping places of Cambridge town parishes. The new St Michael's was planned to carry out this double purpose, and its fourteenth-century architecture is of high quality. The southern aisle, with a beautiful founder's chapel, was made over to Michaelhouse, while the scholars of Gonville Hall used that on the northern side. The unusually short nave contained the people of a parish whose lay population may have been de-clining as its academic inhabitants increased. It seems that the large chancel may have been ordered 'collegewise' for the inmates of the first College to use the church. But I doubt whether the 36 stalls still in the chancel of St Michael's were made for the combined use of Michaelhouse and Gonville Hall, for they were brought from Trinity chapel, early in the eighteenth century, to help make way for those put in by Bentley. I think it more likely that they are those set up, about 1485, in the newly completed chapel of King's Hall.

Some sets of rooms were built at various times in Michaelhouse's history, and by 1425 the College possessed a library. Later still there were buildings which gave it more of the appearance one now associates with a well-established and comfortably endowed collegiate foundation. A gate tower led in from the northern end of Milne Street (Trinity Hall Lane). Then, in the early years of the sixteenth century, a generous benefaction made it possible for the College to build what must, at that time, have been one of the finest halls in Cambridge. Its oriel window, projecting on a trefoiled plan which was like that of windows in Thornbury Castle, and in the Suffolk mansion of Hengrave Hall, was in the top flight of early Tudor architecture. The style of Michaelhouse's new hall was more accomplished than the debased late Elizabethan Gothic used by Trinity for most of the rest of Great Court. The hall was big enough to serve, for over fifty years, as the Hall of the far larger foundation of Trinity; its noble oriel survived, in front of Trinity's buttery, till the 1770s. Its screens passage was on the same alignment as that of the present hall of Trinity. I think it not unlikely, from the late medieval Perpendicular idiom of the two archways which still lead into the screens passage, that they are not Elizabethan work but the doorways once used, on their way into hall, by the inmates of Michaelhouse.

On the whole, the history of Michaelhouse seems to have been uneventful during the two centuries of the College's existence. Two of its fifteenth-century Masters became bishops, one of Salisbury and the other of Carlisle and then of Chichester. The greatest figure associated with the College was John Fisher, a Michaelhouse graduate who was Master of the College for a few years from 1497. He was the University's Chancellor in 1504 and then, as Bishop of Rochester and Lady Margaret Beaufort's executor, he was the man who helped her with the founding of Christ's and carried out her wishes for the establishment of St John's. In 1535 he was executed for his resistance to Henry VIII's declaration of spiritual supremacy over the English Church. It was for this act of defiance that he was made a Cardinal just before his death, and was canonised in Rome four centuries later.

CLARE

WITHIN two years of the opening of Michaelhouse, and before the tragic end of Edward II's reign, the next Cambridge collegiate foundation had come into being. We here have another story whose historic origins lie earlier than an official foundation date, and the year 1326 is not the first in the history of the academic institution which in the end took root and flourished as Clare Hall.

In the early years of the fourteenth century private benefactions were still the main impetus behind the foundation and endowment of new colleges. But the idea now grew that the University itself (in the persons of the Chancellor and the scholars) should do as had been modestly done at Oxford and be responsible for the running of some endowed habitation for those who came to Cambridge in search of higher learning.

Dr A. C. Chibnall, in his book 'Richard de Badew and the University of Cambridge', has well described the early moves behind the starting of University Hall which was Clare's direct predecessor. It was in 1321 that Roger de Northburgh, a prominent figure in the University who was next year made Bishop of Coventry and Lichfield, got a licence for the University (now papally confirmed as a *Studium Generale*) to hold endowments for the permanent support of a house which would accommodate men studying such subjects as logic and theology. Northburgh's promotion to his bishopric soon removed him from the Cambridge scene. But his idea survived. The site of Clare College, in the old parish of St John Zachary and owned for some years by the University, contained two houses which were already hostels for an informal group of graduates.

In 1325 Bishop Salmon of Norwich gave them a large sum of money, and then in the next year the Northburgh idea was carried out by the endowed

24

CLARE. The Bridge, by Thomas Grumbold, 1639–40

PEMBROKE. The Chapel Façade, by Christopher Wren, 1663–65

establishment, on this particular site, of University Hall. The man responsible was Richard de Badew, a prominent graduate and the University's Chancellor. He was, however, a less wealthy cleric than the founder of Michaelhouse. He was unable to do more, financially speaking, for the new *collegium*, and it got little help from the University which might well have been expected to forward its cause. Badew soon underwent certain financial and political reverses which were unfortunate for the new foundation.

In 1336 only ten of the fifteen Fellows allowed for were actually on the books. It is in this year that we first hear of assistance from the rich, aristocratic, and perhaps somewhat imperious patroness who soon gave the little college its new name. The benefactress who rescued the struggling University Hall was Elizabeth, a daughter and coheiress of Gilbert de Clare, the sixth Earl of Gloucester, and the sister of the young seventh Earl who, in 1314, was killed at Bannockburn. She had been three times widowed, the first and most distinguished of her three husbands having been John de Burgh, heir of the Earl of Ulster. She had large estates, and was anxious to spend some of her great wealth on such good causes as University education. The help she gave in 1336 was followed, in another two years, by extra endowments, and in the next two years University Hall came wholly into the control of Lady Clare (as she now called herself).

It was only in 1346, when the Master and Fellows were in complete possession and quite separate from the University, that she gave it extra endowments so as to bring its income to a reasonable sum. Unlike University College at Oxford, this college lost its original title in favour of the maiden name of its new patroness, and one notes that its arms are those of Clare impaling de Burgh. Lady Clare lived until 1360, and in the year before her death she gave the Clare Hall some pioneering and enlightened new statutes which provided for the presence in the college of poor boys— the forerunners of the modern undergraduate—as well as for graduate residents. Her bequest to the college of the fine ornaments of her private chapel made it possible for Clare Hall to think in terms of a chapel of its own instead of making sole use of the church of St John Zachary. A Papal licence for such a chapel was soon obtained, but St John's was still used for the college burials. Only when this church was demolished to help clear the site for King's did Clare and Trinity Hall move their burials to chapels specially built for them at St Edward's. This was also the time when the comparatively humble, two-storeyed court of Clare Hall became somewhat less shut in, on its southern side, than it had been for the first hundred years of its history. There were, however, no signs as yet of the spacious lawn of King's which now lies close to Clare's Renaissance buildings.

Not much is known of the pre-Reformation history of Clare. Soon after 1521 the chapel was rebuilt, with a library above it, and it was in the early 1520s that Hugh Latimer, not yet aligned with the religious Reformers, was a Fellow of the College. By now there had been a decline in the University's study of civil law, and as this subject had been pursued both in Clare and in its neighbour, Trinity Hall, an unfulfilled proposal was made to amalgamate the two colleges to accommodate the reduced number of civil lawyers.

The Elizabethan period saw comparative tranquillity at Clare. By contrast, the seventeenth century was a time of great activity, not least in the almost complete rebuilding of the college and the creation of most of the harmonious Gothic-cum-Renaissance court which exists today. The new buildings, at first more 'Gothic Survival' in appearance than they are now, were set back from the line of what had once been Milne Street, and lay a little to the west of the position of the medieval court.

After a sharp controversy with King's some ground in Butt Close was also obtained across the river. Hence, on the east of the present Old Court, the space between the main entrance and Trinity Hall Lane; and on the other side the beautiful structure of Clare Bridge which gave the college easy access to its new territory.

The whole process of rebuilding, from the 1630s to the early years of the eighteenth century, had its reasonably close parallel in St Catharine's. Work started in 1638, before the Civil War, in which Clare's sympathies, like those of most Cambridge colleges, were staunchly on the Royalist side. Much of the new work, including the hall and the lovely pilastered river façade, was done after the Restoration. By this time, with Robert Grumbold as the supervising mason–designer in place of John Westley, the style and detail of the new blocks was more completely of the classical Renaissance. Clare's studies lay largely in law, medicine, and divinity, and an important Fellow of the college in the middle years of the seventeenth century was John Tillotson, who was Archbishop of Canterbury for a few years under William and Mary.

In the eighteenth century Clare Hall remained a small college. It also tended to be exclusive, for the sons of some important Whig aristocrats came there as undergraduates. Pelhams, Cornwallises, and Townshends were among them, and there was also Lord Hervey, the polished courtier and the author of brilliantly scathing memoirs of Court life under George II. Sir Horace Mann, the faithful correspondent of Horace Walpole, was also a Clare man, so too was Thomas Pelham Holles, eventually the Duke of Newcastle on Tyne, the supreme behind-the-scenes manipulator in Hanoverian politics and also, as the University's Chancellor, a powerful figure in Cambridge.

Another Clare connection at this time was with colonial America. Nicholas Ferrar, an eminent Clare man of the previous century, had been important as a pioneer supporter of colonial ventures in Virginia, as well as for his religious activities and for his famous community at Little Gidding. Now, in the eighteenth century, the sons of several eminent colonial Americans made their way to Clare; their families included some which achieved prominence in the struggle for American Independence.

The main architectural relic of these Georgian decades is the beautiful classical chapel with its domed and octagonal vestibule.

The first half of the nineteenth century saw Clare Hall in a placid spell. Dr William Webb became Master in 1815, a little over a month after Waterloo. The college saw but one more election to its Mastership before the spring which included the Gallipoli campaign.

Webb was a poor financier and, as he would admit no undergraduates above the number that could find rooms in Clare's single court, the college's inmates remained few, with only forty undergraduates in residence at the beginning of Queen Victoria's reign. One could say, at this time, that Clare was something of a backwater in a Cambridge that was now vigorously expanding. More significant for its future had been the events of 1804, when the awards under the Enclosure of Cambridge Field gave it eleven acres, west of the river, which included the eventual sites both of the present University Library and of Clare's own Memorial Court.

Those who still remember Dr Edward Atkinson as Master of Clare must think of him as a venerable figure, older than almost anyone who has ever been head of a Cambridge college, maintaining what Mansfield Forbes called a state of 'aloof dignity' as a virtual recluse in his beautiful Master's Lodge. His Mastership, of fifty-nine years and two months, took him far into his nineties, and was the longest ever held by the head of a college in Cambridge.

It was not unnatural, at so great an age, that Dr Atkinson resisted change in his later years. He had, however, been only thirty-seven when he took over the post. At that time, when the Crimean War was still being fought, he had been a man of new, progressive ideas. It symbolised the change from Webb to Atkinson that 1856 was the year when Clare Hall, free to make a change denied to Trinity Hall, its northern neighbour, but similar to that also made by Pembroke and Catharine Halls, altered its designation to the more high-sounding one of Clare College.

In the first, and more vigorous part of his Mastership, Dr Atkinson was three times Vice-Chancellor; we are told that he personally audited all the University accounts. Clare College remained a small unit in the University, for all its activities were contained within its one court, and it was among the few Cambridge colleges which throughout the nineteenth century made no additions to its buildings. But forward moves were more in the air when in the last years of the Atkinson régime William Loudon Mollison was an active and energetic college tutor.

But little could be done till after the First World War, and in the early 1920s the college had some difficulty in filling its modest number of vacancies. It was, however, at about this time, with new buildings and tutorship of Mr (later Sir) Henry Thirkill that a more dynamic phase of Clare's history set in. If Clare was to keep pace with the much expanded colleges of twentieth-century Cambridge it needed to increase its undergraduate members. This could only be properly done by the putting up of new buildings. The college's coming sexcentenary, and a natural desire to commemorate the Clare men who died in the First World War, combined to give the needed opportunity. No new buildings could be fitted into the college's ancient site. The physical expansion in Clare occurred in two places. One of these, a piece of college property on the southern slope of Castle Hill, was used for the building of a new hostel.

But the college's most spectacular effort was made on a part of its property beyond the Backs and across Queen's Road. It was here that Clare became the first Cambridge college to house undergraduates so far to the West of the river; the college was thus a pioneer in a movement which has had many recent followers. The Memorial Court of Clare was designed by Sir Giles Gilbert Scott. Its style, with some pleasant touches of detail, is the neo-Georgian much favoured between the wars. It forms a group with the slightly later University Library, built west of it on land sold by Clare for this purpose. The main contrast between the two buildings lies in the colouring of their brickwork—reddish brown for the library, a somewhat insipid greyish mauve for the Memorial Court.

With the new buildings under way, Clare could expand into a college of considerable size. As in other colleges, more scientists than before were among its undergraduates, but then as now Clare maintained a reasonably even balance between the subjects read by its members. In the years between the wars most Clare men came from various public schools. One got the impression that it was certainly favoured by Marlburians, and this was certainly among the schools with which special recruiting contacts were maintained. But no particular preference was in fact shown by Clare to any one public school, and some in the Midlands, such Rasepton, Oundle,

Oakham and Uppingham were also well represented. The college now had a considerable reputation for its rowing prowess.

Since 1945 Clare has had several of the experiences common to Cambridge colleges in the middle rank of size. Its undergraduate numbers, now about three hundred and thirty, have been more than they were before the war, and as in other colleges Clare's post-graduate and research members have increased greatly over the last pre-war figure. Rooms other than the hall itself have had to be used for communal eating which is in any case more important than it was.

The Memorial Court has been extended, in a style similar to the work done earlier by Sir Giles Scott, by a portion named Thirkill Court after the late Sir Henry Thirkill. Much money for this building came from an American Clare man, Mr Paul Mellon, and one notes that a new building which contains about a third of the accommodation found in Memorial Court cost about as much.

Then in 1957–58 Clare gave Cambridge an excellent piece of truly modern college architecture in its Wilflete Hostel (named after a fifteenth-century Master) which Mr David Roberts designed for erection on the college's sloping site below Castle Hill.

More recent developments have included great alterations in the College's eating arrangements, and its admission of female undergraduates. The basement below the hall has been ingeniously converted into a cafeteria and the dining rooms associated with it; one of the dining rooms links directly with the attractive Junior Combination Room which is in the crypt space below the antechapel and the chapel. At lunch time members of Girton College have the right to use this new cafeteria at Clare. In the evening it is reserved for Clare's own members who can also, if they wish, dine more formally in the old hall upstairs. This change has meant that there is only a single session of hall; Clare has thus, in the 1970s, come closer to the dining arrangements which were normal in all Colleges before their great expansion in the nineteenth century.

A greater historic change, and one which would have surprised, and perhaps shocked, the Countess who set University Hall on its new career, has been the admission of female undergraduates. Thirty-eight women came up to Clare in the autumn of 1972, being housed in a group of adjacent staircases in the Memorial Court. Clare's female undergraduates have the same tutors as the men in the College, but two women fellows, appointed some time back, are there to help with their personal problems.

Clare was also, in the 1960s, immersed in a new venture which has brought another Cambridge College into being. The problem which Clare helped to solve applies widely in modern Cambridge, and has been tackled in various ways.

The last few years have seen a fantastic growth in the number of graduate and research workers living in Cambridge. In 1938 the research students on the register numbered 411, with 231 of them resident. In 1964 the equivalent figures were 1,854 and 1,300. By 1972 the total had risen to about 2,500. Many of the post-graduates now in Cambridge are comparatively young men or women who are University employees, not necessarily Cambridge graduates but in such posts as those of demonstrators in the scientific departments. Others are scholars from outside Cambridge, of established eminence and holding teaching posts or engaged in higher research. It has been found that few of these post-graduates can get Fellowships at the older Colleges, while some of those who are not Cambridge men or women have no footing in any College at all. So much have things changed since the earliest, non-collegiate days of the *Studium Generale* at Cambridge that one is somewhat lost and disembodied if one is connected with the University and yet is without a College in which to dine and have some social meeting point. The older Colleges have been able to contain most of the younger research workers and have now provided them with separate parlours or common rooms. But they cannot do all that is socially necessary to give collegiate homes to the more senior post-graduates, men and women, from this country or abroad, who are now so numerous in Cambridge. For these people new endowments, and new collegiate foundations, have come into being.

In 1964 Clare College therefore came forward with a plan, which in two more years it got approved by the University Senate, for the creation of an 'Approved Foundation' which has now blossomed out, on its site in Herschel Road, as a separate College for graduate men and women. Clare Hall, as it is called, has in this book a section of its own on its early, formative years.

PEMBROKE

THOUGH nine years lay between the refounding of Clare and the formal constitution of Pembroke, the early connection of these two Colleges was closer than one might think. Both of them started within that crucial half century which saw more College founding at Cambridge than at Oxford. Another link between them lay in the circumstances, the personalities, and the mutual friendship of the two great ladies who set them on their way.

The foundress of Pembroke was Marie de Valence, *née* Marie de St Pol of a rich and aristocratic family in northern France. She was related to the French royal House, and like Lady Clare she also had in her veins the royal blood of England. Her husband, like herself a relative of England's Plantagenet kings, had been Aymer de Valence, Earl of Pembroke and a close adherent of Edward II. His death in 1324 made Lady Pembroke a widow after less than three years of married life. She never remarried, and lived to what was, in those days, the great age of nearly eighty. In the later years of her life she was a great helper of religious and charitable causes. She was a special patroness of the Franciscan friars and nuns, and it was in 1342 that she founded the Franciscan nunnery at Denny between Cambridge and Ely. In the same year, so we find from the article on Pembroke College in the third volume of the 'Victoria County History of Cambridge and Ely', she bought the first part of what soon became the site of Pembroke College.

Lady Pembroke, in her desire to help those pursuing their studies at Cambridge, may well have been inspired and influenced by Lady Clare. The two widowed countesses were close friends, and as Lady Clare was still active in her work for her College at the time when Lady Pembroke was thinking about her own foundation in Cambridge one imagines the two ladies discussing their schemes over the fourteenth-century equivalent of tea and dainty sandwiches. One also notes, in the early arrangements for Pembroke, that its members, like those of Clare Hall, were to include boys, at the undergraduate level, as well as the senior scholars or Fellows.

However long Lady Pembroke may have spent over the preliminaries to the foundation of her College, the task was accomplished by the end of 1347. Edward III signed the foundation Charter on Christmas Eve of that year. The Hall of Valence Marie, or Pembroke Hall as it was soon called, could now set out on its long academic career. The foundress gradually extended the site, and the small, compact court of the original College was built in the middle decades of the century. Where Pembroke created a precedent was in the early possession of its own chapel. Though at first the scholars of Pembroke Hall worshipped in St Botolph's church the Countess got a Papal Licence, in 1355, for her College to have its own chapel, available for all purposes and without the partial use of any parish church. Pembroke thus became the first Cambridge College to enjoy this facility within its own walls.

For the rest of the fourteenth century and somewhat later the numbers at Pembroke Hall seem not to have reached the thirty scholars allowed for by the foundress; only nine Fellows and a boy were in residence in 1412. Later in the Lancastrian period, under Henry VI, Pembroke Hall came much into favour. Its endowments were much increased by grants from the confiscated property of some 'alien' priories which had belonged to abbeys in France, and several of the College's masters and Fellows became bishops. John Langton, who became Master of Pembroke in 1428 and was also the Chancellor of the University, was among those who persuaded Henry VI to found King's. William Booth, a Pembroke man, became Archbishop of York in 1452. His half brother Laurence, a staunch Lancastrian, was a great benefactor to the College when he too was its Master. He also concluded his ecclesiastical career as the holder of the northern archbishopric.

The events of Pembroke Hall's first century and a half lay well within the limits of medieval orthodoxy, while by the end of the Middle Ages the College was better endowed than most others in Cambridge. Northcountrymen were still strong among its members, and it was a Northumbrian Fellow, Nicholas Ridley, who was the leading Pembroke man among the early Reformers. Though Pembroke, like other Colleges, was divided in its religious sympathies its Fellows in time included a Reformist majority.

Ridley became Master in 1540 and raised the College's reputation as a stronghold of Reform. His mastership, held jointly with the bishoprics of Rochester and then of London, ended with his burning at Oxford in 1555. In his farewell to his old College he touchingly called Pembroke 'studious, well learned, and a great setter forth of Christ's gospel and of God's true word'. For the rest of the Tudor period, and in the seventeenth century as well, the College was still eminent for the number of Pembroke men who became archbishops or bishops.

Pembroke's most distinguished Tudor man of letters was Edmund Spenser, who came up in 1569. Pembroke's strongly Protestant, even Puritan character was modified from 1589, the year in which Lancelot Andrewes became Master. Andrewes was prominent as a staunch High Churchman, and under his régime a 'Laudian' and royalist complexion came over Pembroke Hall. In the early years of the seventeenth century the College was of a fair size, with its members numbering about 120 around 1616. By then, however, the mastership of Samuel Harsnett (later Archbishop of York) had been a time of unhappy dispute, largely because, as the Master was already a bishop, he was often away from Cambridge. Pembroke's mainly royalist sympathies continued after Harsnett had resigned, and until the time of the Civil War. Ecclesiastics apart, a Pembroke man of this period was also a poet of considerable merit.

Richard Crashaw was a Pembroke graduate, but soon moved over the street to Peterhouse; his migration was just the opposite of that later achieved by Thomas Gray. At the time of the Civil War Crashaw was ejected from his Peterhouse Fellowship, became a Roman Catholic, and died in Italy.

The leading Pembroke man of the seventeenth century was Matthew Wren, important not only in his own right but for the influence and patronage which gave chances as an architect to his nephew Christopher. Matthew Wren first came up when Lancelot Andrewes was Master, and as President of the College he was much concerned with the building of the homely first block of Ivy Court. Though he became Master not of Pembroke but of Peterhouse it was to his original College that his great benefaction went. A Royalist College like Pembroke could hardly fail, with the victory of the Puritan cause, to see most of its Fellows ejected, and in 1645 Richard Vines became Master of an almost empty College. But Pembroke's prosperity improved before the Restoration, and the 'Hitcham' block, started in the 1650s, was almost the only building in any Cambridge College to be commenced under the Commonwealth. Then in 1663 Matthew Wren, restored to his Ely bishopric and anxious to make some notable thank-offering for the reversal of the Stuart and Anglican fortunes, gave his old College its most important building.

The rectangular chapel, mainly of brick but with a pilastered classical façade in lovely stonework, was designed by Christopher Wren and started in 1663; Loggan's print of 1688 shows it with a clock face just above its western window. It was not, strictly speaking, Wren's earliest work of architecture, for the more structurally significant Sheldonian Theatre at Oxford was designed a little earlier and was started at about the same time. Pembroke's chapel was, however, the first Wren building to be actually finished. The building which had been the chapel pioneeringly built by Lady Pembroke duly became the College library, and it was one of the plasterers who worked under Wren in London, a fine craftsmen named Henry Doogood, who made the splendid ceiling with its date of 1690. Sir Christopher retained his interest in the College, for his son, the third Christopher Wren, came up there in 1691.

From about 1653, and for much of the eighteenth century, Pembroke's membership was in one respect more what one would associate with Exeter College, Oxford. For many of its entrants, and some who attained distinction, came from Cornwall. The connection probably arose from the long ministry in the Duchy of a Pembroke Fellow who took a Cornish living.

For most of the Georgian period Pembroke was a strongly Tory College. One gets the impression of a small, friendly, and agreeable society. But its peace was troubled, in the 1740s, by a sharp dispute between the Fellows and Roger Long, the eccentric Master, which on its smaller scale recalled the great battle in Trinity just ended by the death of Bentley. Undergraduate numbers now dropped sharply, but they duly revived, and the Pembroke high table remained sociable and pleasant. The poet Gray, unhappy in his residence at Peterhouse across the street, had many Pembroke friends before his famous migration of 1756. Pembroke Hall was his main place of residence until his death. His happiness there, amid congenial company, serves to remind us that in those days of unmarried dons a College, much more than nowadays, could command from a resident Fellow the affection one feels for home. Gray died in College in 1771; in another two years the young William Pitt came up, to become the most politically eminent of all Pembroke men.

From 1784, for a spell of 86 years, Pembroke had two of the excessively long masterships which were all too common in eighteenth-century Cambridge, and also during the Victorian age which eventually saw large measures of University and College reform. Joseph Turner, who for much of his time of office was also Dean of Norwich, reigned for 44 years, and Gilbert Ainslie for 42 till his death in 1870. During Turner's time Pembroke remained a very small College, nor indeed had it the space or buildings for real expansion, the eighteenth century having been a time when the College had done very little building work.

But Ainslie, with an eye for expansion which never actually came in his time, was energetic in his policy of increasing the area of the College. He also did valuable work on its records, and obtained new statutes granted in 1844. From then onward he was increasingly caught up in the deep problems which arose from the obvious need for University and College reform. Himself in favour of changes, he was none the less saddened by the way in which they came about not so much from within the University as from a Royal Commission and Parliamentary action. The numbers, and the academic standards, of Pembroke remained modest in his time, and no new buildings arose on the ground he had wisely bought.

It was under Ainslie's successor that there occurred the sad demolition of one range of the foundress' court and of her College's medieval hall, and the building of Waterhouse's unattractive mid-Victorian blocks. Though they gave Pembroke much valuable space, making it possible for the College's numbers to rise threefold, they are among the least pleasing College buildings in Cambridge. Ironically enough, some money for their building came from a fund slowly raised to commemorate Gray, whose sensitive Augustan taste would surely have been outraged by their style. Far better than these Waterhouse buildings were the chapel's extension and the New Court of 1882, both designed by the younger George Gilbert Scott.

Since the 1880s Pembroke College has grown greatly in numbers and distinction, and its undergraduate numbers reached 250 in the first years of this century. Evangelical clergy and members of the Indian Civil Service were for a time prominent among Pembroke men, while the College's peak period of athletic success was largely a matter of the four decades after 1900. As in other Colleges, those reading scientific subjects have become a larger element than was ever thought likely in the past. During the second World War Pembroke, partly occupied by men doing their initial training for the Royal Air Force, was the only Cambridge College to see its buildings much damaged. But the fire was of the ordinary type, and not due to enemy bombing. Repairs made it possible to improve the accommodation in the damaged block, and Pembroke, like some other Colleges, has gained extra sleeping room by the doubling of single sets. Its one post-war range of buildings shows marked stylistic conservatism.

Pembroke's 700th anniversary was kept quietly in 1947, and since that year the College's story has contained many features found elsewhere in Cambridge. Athletic achievement, though kept up at a good average level, is less outstanding now than it was before the war, while those reading natural and mechanical sciences are relatively far more numerous in Pembroke than they were before 1939. English has remained a strong subject in the College, whose undergraduates now number about 330. Pembroke's

Fellows and research Fellows have greatly increased in the 1960s, and the College now has a notably young, and recently elected high table. Lords Butler and Plowden are among the most eminent of living Pembroke men, while the cricketing exploits of Peter May were in tune with the College's tradition of sporting eminence. The renovation and cleaning of the Waterhouse block, with the revelation of its architect's sculptural detail and bright High Victorian colour scheme, has been followed by restoration work on the Wren chapel, and by the renovation and improvement of the rooms in the younger George Gilbert Scott's New Court.

GONVILLE AND CAIUS

FROM Pembroke we move on to three colleges, founded in the same century yet different in their background from the first four which were started in the years after 1300. From colleges whose origins reflect the complex politics of Edward II's reign, and the personalities and ideals of highly placed personages at the Plantagenet Court, we turn to those whose founders were practical, hard-headed clerics or laymen, planning their ventures in Cambridge to meet the ecclesiastical needs of their time.

An obvious requirement, in the first half of the fourteenth century, was that for a better supply of educated secular (i.e. non-monastic) clergy. It was to help meet that need that Edmund Gonville, himself a secular priest and the holder of various livings in the diocese of Norwich as well as some civilian appointments, arranged for the foundation of a small College in Cambridge. Unlike the founder of Michaelhouse, Gonville was not personally wealthy. But he seems to have had access to ample funds, and in his scheme for Gonville Hall he was helped by the friendship and counsel of his bishop, William Bateman, who held the see of Norwich from 1344 to 1355, and who was already planning to found his own Cambridge college of Trinity Hall.

The first site of Gonville Hall was some distance from the present Caius College. For the founder bought some houses in Lurthburgh (now Free School) Lane, between that lane and the site now filled by the Wilkins Court of Corpus Christi College. It was there, after getting a licence in January, 1348, that Gonville first placed his endowed foundation. Its members, mostly on higher studies in dialectic and theology, were to be a Master and twenty Fellows. Events soon caused the move of the little college to a different site.

The year 1348–49 was that of the Black Death, with England severely hit by the worst of its medieval outbreaks of bubonic plague. Deaths were specially numerous among the parish clergy, and we know that in East Anglia the mortality among the parish priests was particularly high. Special steps, such as the founding of new colleges, had obviously to be taken to replenish their ranks. Bishop Bateman, with the clergy of his diocese much reduced by the pestilence, had a special interest in any measures which might help him in a serious pastoral crisis. Then, in 1351, Edmund Gonville died; like Bishop Balsham at Peterhouse, but unlike Ladies Clare and Pembroke, he was not spared long enough to set his new foundation far on its way.

Gonville's friend Bishop Bateman was the man who decisively changed the early story of Gonville Hall. In 1350, and on the site it has always held, he had founded Trinity Hall. His purpose, in creating a college whose main studies were to lie in civil and canon law, was to replenish the ranks of his better instructed parish clergy.

The same idea, at a time when such men were pressingly needed, lay behind Gonville's foundation. The two colleges, both of them with a strong East Anglian orientation, could complement each other. Bishop Bateman now saw his obvious chance to control them both. Such a policy would be made easier by their physical nearness. So Bateman moved Gonville Hall to a site close to that of his own college; he thereby made things easier for the founders of Corpus Christi College, whose scheme was now being actively discussed. Had he left Gonville Hall in Lurthburgh Lane the history and the physical growth both of Caius and Corpus Christi would have been very different.

Bishop Bateman bought Gonville's scholars two substantial houses along the southern side of St Michael's (now Trinity) Lane. They, and the ground behind them, accounted for the site now covered by Gonville Court in the much larger college of Gonville and Caius. During the rest of the fourteenth and fifteenth centuries the remainder of Gonville Court was slowly built. The chapel, which was finished by 1393, was a pioneering building in Cambridge in that its clunch walls were faced with brick. Bishop Bateman also gave Gonville Hall new statutes, and to mark its close connection with his own college a 'Treaty of Amity' between Gonville and Trinity Halls was made in 1353.

The bishop also provided that Edmund Gonville's Fellows could study civil and canon law, and also medicine, as well as theology. His death in 1355 affected the development of Gonville's foundation as well as that of his own. For the rest of the Middle Ages Gonville Hall's endowments increased but little, and its Fellows were always less than half of the twenty provided for by the founder.

Another, and long-enduring feature of the college, was its strongly entrenched connection with the East Anglian counties of the diocese of Norwich. It was thus no surprise that in the fifteenth century Gonville Hall got some valuable benefactions from prominent citizens of Norwich. The Cathedral Priory of Norwich was also a source of new residents at Gonville Hall. For from 1481 student monks from this, and other Benedictine monasteries in East Anglia, came to reside in the college while studying at Cambridge.

Early in the sixteenth century Gonville Hall had some thirty to forty residents, nearly half of them in the now increasing class of pensioners, or fee-paying students. Not unnaturally, the student monks and the advocates of religious changes became opposed groups in the little college as the time of the Reformation drew near. The middle years of the sixteenth century found Gonville Hall's members more aligned with the Reformers than with the Catholic partisans; it was ironic that its refoundation and increased standing came from a staunch supporter of the older ways.

John Keys (or Caius as he Latinised his name in the typical Renaissance manner) was a Norwich man, a graduate of Gonville Hall, and a Fellow of the College. He studied medicine at the famous University of Padua, and on his return became a prominent, well-patronised physician in London. It was in 1557, when Mary I was on the throne and when Catholic prospects in England seemed reasonably bright, that he became his old college's most important benefactor. He obtained for it the charter of foundation it had lacked before, doubled its endowments, and added his own highly symbolic arms to those of Gonville to make up the new coat of what now became Gonville and Caius College. In 1559, despite the recent accession of Elizabeth I, he became its Master.

While holding that office he added to its site, and built Caius Court whose open southern side was so planned as to admit to its enclosed space a good breath of healthy fresh air. Its style, as one still sees, blended Tudor Gothic with Renaissance classicism of the type Caius would have seen in and near Padua.

The years of Caius's Mastership were, however, soured by the sharp religious and personal differences between him and the Fellows. Things came to a head when, at the end of 1572, his lodge was sacked, with the destruction of many vestments and other Catholic ornaments which Dr Caius had reverently secreted. Broken-hearted, he resigned his Mastership next year and died soon after.

Dr Caius's successor was Thomas Legge, who had been a popular tutor at Jesus College. Though a more definite Anglican than Caius, he was enough in sympathy with the old religion for the college, in his time as Master, to see the unusual phenomenon of many entrants from among the families of 'Recusant' gentry, particularly in Yorkshire. Several Caius men of the Elizabethan period became Jesuits or secular seminary priests, while five suffered death for their Catholicism in Elizabeth's reign. By the end of the century the Roman Catholic element at Caius had declined.

From now onwards, and in sympathy with the profession of its second founder, the college increased its standing as a centre of medical studies. Stephen Perse, M.D., the founder of the Perse School in Cambridge, was an eminent Caius man of this period, and his school on its first site in Free School Lane was long controlled by the Master and Fellows of Gonville and Caius College.

Caius College, like most others in Cambridge, was Royalist in sympathy at the time of the Civil War. However, its growing preoccupation with medical studies made it less theological in tone than some other colleges, and therefore less likely to be deeply committed in the great controversies of those times. Despite the eventual ejection of its Master and of several Fellows, it seems that the Parliamentary régime meant less of an upheaval in Caius than in some other colleges. New buildings, of brick-faced clunch and in a simple Jacobean Gothic style, had been put up with funds left by Drs Legge and Perse, and in the years just before the Civil War Caius was a large unit among the colleges of Cambridge and stood about third or fourth in the number of its inmates. Its East Anglian connection, and its medical traditions, continued after the Restoration. Two contemporaries as medical students at Caius in the 1680s were Thomas Dover, later well known as the inventor of Dover's powder, and Elias Daffy who made his name known with Daffy's elixir.

The eighteenth-century story of Caius was one of considerable decline, and of an East Anglian dominance even greater than that which had already prevailed. Over seven-eighths of those coming to Caius at this time were Norfolk or Suffolk men, and most of them went back to their native counties as clergy or members of the squirearchy. Very typical of this connection was the Rev. Edmund Nelson, of a family related to the Walpoles and with a typically East Anglian Christian name. He entered the college in 1741, took his B.A. degree in 1745, and for two years from 1751 was a Junior Fellow. By now he had married, and soon settled down to his long tenure of the Norfolk living of Burnham Thorpe, in whose parsonage the victor of the Nile and Trafalgar was born. More distinguished Caius men of this

TRINITY HALL. The Old Library, c. 1580, from the garden

CORPUS CHRISTI. Old Court; St Benet's tower behind

period ended their academic careers as Masters of the college. One of these was Thomas Gooch, an active and capable Master and also, as Vice-Chancellor, a prominent antagonist of Bentley. Not long before he died he inherited a baronetcy, and he held his Mastership of Caius along with the bishoprics of Norwich and then of Ely. His successor, Sir James Burrough, was well known in Cambridge as an amateur architect in the Palladian style. The inner refacing and rewindowing of Gonville Court was by him. Later in the eighteenth century, the old hall was elegantly refitted by the architect Soane, and with this work the original buildings of Gonville Hall lost the remaining traces of their medieval appearance.

A Caius man of the later Georgian period who achieved distinction as an architect was William Wilkins, at first an exponent of pure Grecian classicism, but later a prolific worker in the neo-Perpendicular of the early Gothic revival. This revived Gothic was the style suggested by Wilkins, in 1822, for new buildings in Tree Court for what was now a reviving and expanding college. Important work was, however, postponed until well into the Victorian age. The principal Victorian buildings put up in Caius were Salvin's new hall and the unlovely blocks by Waterhouse which more than replaced the modest Jacobean ranges named after Drs Legge and Perse.

The blue gown which lends distinction to the appearance of Caius men had been adopted in the year of Queen Victoria's accession.

In the mid-Victorian decades the college's religious tone was mainly evangelical, while in 1860 its new statutes put an end to the special position enjoyed in the college by men from East Anglia.

From late in the Victorian period one has the modern story of a continually expanding Gonville and Caius college. Prominence on the river in the 1840s opened out into achievements in a wider field of athletics. Medical traditions were well maintained, and the college was still, after Trinity and St John's, one of the larger units in Cambridge. For this reason it could no longer be contained within the site bounded by Trinity Street, Trinity Hall Lane, Trinity Lane and Senate House Passage. So in 1887 it stepped beyond its old boundaries by the purchase, across Trinity Street, of Rose Crescent. The houses on one side of the crescent were adapted as college rooms, and were duly replaced by the buildings of St Michael's Court which envelop the church in whose North aisle the scholars of Gonville Hall originally worshipped. Later still, the southern side of this court was rebuilt so as to combine college sets and income-producing shop property facing out onto Market Hill.

The current history of Caius is in some respects along lines already familiar. With about three hundred and ninety undergraduate members it is among the larger colleges, and as elsewhere in Cambridge one finds many more Fellows than before the war, and a vast increase in the college's post-graduate research workers. Though natural sciences (leading on to medicine) are still apt to be Caius College's most favoured subject there were times, in the 1950s and 1960s, when the Caius men reading engineering outnumbered the college's medics. English literature, hardly studied in Caius in the 1930s, has a respectable following and Caius men have now spread out into several subjects once little regarded in the college.

A fine undergraduate reading room has been made out of three college sets, and a geographical move, more far-reaching than the short hop across Trinity Street, has been made by the building, across the Backs on part of the site of the new Fellows' Garden, of Sir Leslie Martin's Harvey Court. This gives the much-transformed College of Edmund Gonville and John Caius new accommodation for what they would have considered the extremely large number of about 100 undergraduates.

No more new buildings have been started, but some extra living accomodation will come from the renovation and reheating of the Waterhouse building which is now in hand. More spectacular recent improvements are the new kitchens and the splendid redecoration of the Victorian hall, while a strikingly decorated coffee bar, with cloakrooms and an exhibition room below it, has been fitted out in the north-western corner of the ancient Gonville Court. An institutional change has come with the setting up, for purposes of consultation, of an academic committee with a half-and-half ratio of senior and junior members.

TRINITY HALL

VERY soon after Edmund Gonville had founded his little endowed hall in Lurthburgh Lane, and at the time when that college was still at work on its original site, Gonville's diocesan bishop and close friend William Bateman had launched his own college of Trinity Hall. The college's foundation deed is dated at the beginning of 1350. There must, however, have been some months at least of preliminary work and discussion.

We may assume that the Bishop of Norwich's plans, for a college whose graduates in canon and civil law would be useful both to the Church and in affairs of state, went back to the months which immediately followed the Black Death which in 1348 and 1349 wrought such havoc among the trained clergy of his own East Anglian diocese. Bishop Bateman's new college was supposed to provide for twenty Fellows in addition to the Master. All were to pursue higher studies in civil or canon law. But as in some other colleges unexpected events (arising, for Trinity Hall, from its founder's premature death) prevented the full realisation of an original scheme. Yet Trinity Hall can claim that it got well established within its first half-dozen years, and that its buildings have always stood on the site bought at the beginning, and augmented in later years. In 1350 these were between Milne Street (now Trinity Hall Lane) and the river just downstream from the 'back-side' of Clare.

One building already on the site was a house of the Norman period which had been used as a hostel by student monks from the cathedral monastery at Ely; a window of this house, preserved above the panelling of the dais in the college's hall, is one of the oldest pieces of building in any Cambridge college. But most of the existing houses were gradually cleared away and the first court of Trinity Hall was finished, as was that of the almost contemporary college of Corpus Christi, by about 1375. The chapel, like that at

Pembroke, was among the earliest included in the fabric of a college at Cambridge. But for burials, and for some other purposes, the members of Trinity Hall still used the parish church of St John Zachary, and later their specially built chapel at St Edward's.

Bishop Bateman died in 1355, and both Gonville and Trinity Halls were much affected by the loss of their chief patron. At Trinity Hall progress seems to have been modest throughout the time from the fourteenth century to the Reformation, and numbers were certainly small. Though some benefactions came in, the Fellows of the college never, in all that long period, reached the number of twenty provided for by the founder. As with some others among the early Cambridge colleges we know little in detail of the pre-Reformation history of Trinity Hall.

Canonists held most of the fellowships which did exist, but as several of them also studied civil (or Roman) law the founder's purpose of a balance between these two studies was in a manner achieved. Then, under Henry VIII, the prohibition of the study, in England, of canon law had a deep effect on a college whose main purpose, and actual work, had lain in that discipline. Civil law seemed for some years to come to have a great future before it, and there was even a proposal to amalgamate Trinity Hall, along with Clare, its southern neighbour, into a new college for the study of the rising subject.

The leading Trinity Hall man in this time of religious controversy and upheaval was Stephen Gardiner, the lawyer and ecclesiastic who was prominent, in his somewhat devious way, in the political and religious controversies of his time. Despite his acceptance of Henry VIII's supremacy over the English Church, his personal convictions were not Protestant but lay strongly in the Catholic direction. His long tenure of the see of Winchester was interrupted, as were his Mastership of the Hall and his Chancellorship of the University, by a spell of deprivation and imprisonment during the reign of Edward VI.

The last two years of his life saw him back in favour under Mary I. He was, for a time, the leader of the Catholic party and he was the bishop who, in his own cathedral at Winchester, married the Queen to Philip II of Spain. He also did good service to Trinity Hall when he staunchly, and successfully, opposed its amalgamation with Clare. Latimer (a prominent Clare man) and Ridley were equally strong in their fight for Clare, so that religious differences did not stand between these eminent Tudor churchmen in their defence of Cambridge's collegiate *status quo*.

Gardiner was also the Master of the Hall who added to his college's somewhat cramped site the strip of ground which lies between the back of its main court's northern range and the public highway now known as Garret Hostel Lane.

For some three centuries after the accession of Elizabeth I, the story of Trinity Hall was mainly that of a small college whose members largely concentrated on the study of civil law, and on its practice in the courts where it applied. This dualism, between academic life and legal practice, caused the college to differ in some ways from the others which existed in these centuries before the onset of University and college reform. Its Masters were laymen. So, too, were many of its Fellows, and most of those who had active practices in the courts were rarely resident in Cambridge.

The Hall's London property appropriately included Doctors' Commons, which was the stronghold in the capital of those who practised civil law; the allocation of the rooms there was actually controlled by the college. Yet Trinity Hall in time came under a great disadvantage. For civil law failed to maintain the strong position in the English legal system which had seemed destined for it under the early Tudors. Its practice declined, so that a college so biassed towards its study found that its entrants were few, with an annual average, till well on in the Victorian period, of no more than five matriculations. One found, moreover, that more and more Trinity Hall men turned over to the more promising study of the common law. Yet the college was not, in this long period of its small size and academic stagnation, without its notable men.

The late years of Elizabeth I's reign were those in which the Hall built its lovably attractive library block, faced with deep red brick and with its charming step-gabled end. An Elizabethan notable in the college was Dr William Mowse, whose bequest for highway repairs led, in the eighteenth century, to the setting up of the famous series of Trinity Hall milestones along the London road which must have been much used by the Fellows of the college who divided their time between Cambridge and Doctors' Commons.

Dr Eden, the college's Master who died in 1645, was a Parliament sympathiser and the University's Member of Parliament in the Long Parliament. He died in office, and no Fellows of Trinity Hall were ejected under the Commonwealth.

The eighteenth century (when the famous wit, Lord Chesterfield, was a Hall man) saw great changes under the energetic Mastership of Sir Nathaniel Lloyd, and there was a project for the riverward extension of its buildings which would have caused the demolition of the library and would have given the college a dignified Palladian court looking out towards the Granta. As it was, the chapel and the hall were transformed inside, and the inner side of the main court was so refaced that it now has the best and most complete Georgian appearance, as an eighteenth-century veneer on a much older structure, of any court in Cambridge. By about 1750 Trinity Hall had become a serene Augustan haunt for the Fellows who were all too seldom resident within its walls.

It was no surprise, when one saw the final decay of the civil law, and of Doctors' Commons as described by Dickens, that Trinity Hall had little part in Cambridge's first phase of nineteenth-century expansion, and that the college did little building in the years soon after Waterloo which was the time when the novelist Bulwer Lytton was one of its members.

An event of some importance for the college's fortunes, and for an important aspect of Cambridge's scientific studies, was in 1831 when Trinity Hall sold to the University the present site of the Botanic Garden.

Yet the nineteenth century was eventually that of the great transformation which made of Trinity Hall the college one has known in modern times. What hastened the changes was the ending in the 1850s of civil law as a separate branch of legal practice, and the winding up of the long decaying Doctors' Commons. The Common lawyers took over the work long done by the practitioners in civil law, and the numerous Hall men who still read law had finally to turn their attention to common law. Subjects other than law were also studied. The second half of last century saw a spectacular increase in the number of those coming up to Trinity Hall, and the college was, for a few years, the fourth largest in Cambridge. Henry Latham, who was tutor for over thirty years, and Sir Henry Maine, the eminent civil lawyer who ended his career as the college's Master, were leading figures in this period of the Hall's swift change and expansion. This was also the time when Trinity Hall blossomed out as a leading rowing college. New buildings had to be put up to house the larger numbers of Hall men, and the years between 1892 and 1910 saw the gradual building up, along the side of its irregular expanse which lies next to Garret Hostel Lane, of Garden Court which leads down to the river and now opens onto it.

Some aspects of the Hall's Victorian life kept continuity with a past history which had not been that of a 'Laudian' or clerical college. The simple services in its chapel displayed a somewhat typical lawyers' suspicion of 'high' churchmanship, and no organ was used there till after the First World War. The college soon encouraged the entry of Nonconformists, Augustine Birrell being one of them who later achieved political and literary fame. It was also friendly to 'liberalism' in Church affairs, and it was significant that a leading Victorian churchman who hailed from Trinity Hall was Frederick Denison Maurice. Another theological liberal, eventually an agnostic and a central figure in a famous phase of controversy in Cambridge, was Leslie Stephen. For two years he held a Fellowship which provided Trinity Hall with a resident chaplain, but in the end he resigned his Anglican Orders because he could not, as a matter of belief and intellectual integrity, continue as a clergyman.

The completion of the Latham Building's second section brought Trinity Hall close to the years of the First World War, and to the college as one knew it in the years between the wars. It was a prominent rowing college, and one where law was still the largest subject, but where other subjects were also read with real distinction. Little building work was done at this time, and the Hall stayed within the intimate surroundings of the original site as enlarged by Bishop Gardiner.

Since 1945 there have, as in other colleges, been many changes in Trinity Hall. At one time it touched a peak figure of about three hundred and twenty-five undergraduates. But their number is now down to some three hundred, and the college's policy is to keep them round that figure. Law, with some sixty men reading it, remains the largest single subject in Trinity Hall. But it is a new thing in the college's life that engineering and science now come fairly near it. One can see it as a symbol of change that the Hall's Master is Professor Deer, the holder of the University's chair of mineralogy and petrology and the Chairman of the Committee whose report on the long-term needs of the scientific subjects may prove an epoch-making document in the history of modern Cambridge. Some building work, complete by 1964, was the ingenious insertion of a new Senior Combination Room into a space between one end of the hall, the Master's Lodge, and the boundary of Clare.

The last few years have seen the setting up, and useful functioning, of consultative committees, including junior members, which have dealt with such matters as catering and kitchen problems, and with the planning of the College's new buildings near its playing field. The first block, housing 32 undergraduates and two Fellows, is by Arup Associates and is basically similar to one of the blocks in Corpus Christi's post-graduate settlement of Leckhampton. Erected on Trinity Hall's 'Wychfield' property, whose house of 1884 was built by Sir Francis Darwin and figures in 'Period Piece', the new block is one of the best recent buildings in Cambridge. Another one, of similar character and due to contain flats for married graduates, was well advanced, elsewhere in the grounds, by the early days of 1973; its erection is being financed by the development of Trinity Hall property, facing Hills Road, not far from Bateman Street which bears the founder's name.

CORPUS CHRISTI

THE foundation of Corpus Christi College appears, at first sight, to have happened under auspices unlike those which lay behind the other mid-fourteenth-century colleges in Cambridge. Yet one at least of the high personages concerned with the early days of Corpus was involved in another Cambridge College's early history, and the starting of Corpus seems partly to have been in answer to the need which increased the urgency of Edmund Gonville's benefaction and which caused Bishop Bateman to found Trinity Hall.

In the decade which included the founding of Pembroke and Gonville Halls, and which also saw Bishop Bateman working on his early plans, the members of the Cambridge Guilds of Corpus Christi and St Mary got together to found and endow a college of priests. Its inmates were to be enabled to pursue higher studies in theology and canon law, and prayer for the souls of guild members was to be among their obligations. Preparations may have been in progress as far back as 1342; had this year included the actual foundation of Corpus it would now have been the third oldest surviving Cambridge college. The Black Death may in part have caused a delay, so far as formal documents went, of another ten years.

The Corpus Christi Guild had its headquarters in St Benet's Church. It was therefore convenient for the new College to be as near as possible to the building which was long to be its members' place of worship. Some members of the guild owned houses along Lurthburgh (now Free School) Lane south-east of the church. These were pulled down to clear part of the site of Old Court. Some academic hostels were also acquired by the new college, and more ground became available when Bishop Bateman moved Gonville Hall to a site near his own new foundation of Trinity Hall. The complete area of Corpus was thus much larger than that covered by the simple buildings of its original court.

Though the first impetus towards the founding of the new College had come from the Cambridge townsmen in the two guilds some other leading people were also involved. Bishop Bateman, one imagines, was sympathetic.

Sir Walter Manny, a famous soldier and the founder of the London Charter-house, was an early benefactor. The noble patron who got the royal licence for the College's foundation was Henry, Duke of Lancaster, related to Edward III and a soldier of high standing at Court; Edmund Gonville had been steward to him and his father. It must have been easy to interest him in the new academic ventures now much in evidence in Cambridge, and one may say that with Duke Henry there started the Lancastrian impact on Cambridge so conspicuously continued by the Duke's great-grandson King Henry VI.

Corpus Christi College was at first a very small one of a Master and two Fellows. More Fellowships followed as later gifts came in, and in the college's early years all its members were to be in priest's orders. No scholarships for young men were founded for over a hundred years. The first statutes of Corpus were granted in 1356, being largely modelled on those which Hervey de Stanton had given to Michaelhouse.

Things went smoothly for the next twenty-five years. John of Gaunt succeeded his father as the new college's patron, being of service to Corpus in the legal processes whereby its endowments increased in the 1370s. But serious trouble came to Corpus in 1381, that year of widespread insurrection and violent unrest. The national unpopularity of 'time-honoured Lancaster', and the connection of Corpus Christi College with many prosperous guildsmen made it a special target for the Cambridge rioters who disliked the college as the owner of much town property, and of many dues arising within the town. The mob whose members attacked University officials, and destroyed the records of the University itself also broke into Corpus and destroyed the college's records and various items of its property. Substantial damages were recovered after the revolt.

For most of the fifteenth century there is little to record in the history of Corpus. Its first endowed scholarship came in 1489, and soon after that year repairs to its already crumbling clunch buildings were made possible by the generosity of two great ladies whose interest in the college recalls the earlier enthusiasm for Cambridge of Ladies Clare and Pembroke. One of them, Elizabeth, Duchess of Norfolk, was the mother of the little girl Ann Mowbray who was the child bride of the ill-fated Richard Duke of York, and whose remains were lately found in London and re-buried at West-minster. Dr Cosyn, the Master of Corpus from 1487 to 1515, was the Duch-ess's chaplain and a leading figure in the University as a whole. By now the Reformation period was approaching a time when Corpus was somewhat divided in its sympathies and had as a member a leading churchman in the Anglican settlement who was also among its greatest benefactors.

Matthew Parker, born in Norfolk like many Cambridge men of his and later times, came up in 1521. A lover of books and learning, he became a Fellow in 1528 and was chosen Master in 1544. As the head of the college he made numerous physical improvements in the old court, and added a gallery (perhaps like that surviving at Queens') to the Master's Lodge. He was, by now, an ally of the more moderate Reformers.

The beginning of Elizabeth I's reign saw vacancies at Canterbury and in nearly all the other English sees. Parker was chosen for the highest available post, becoming the first, and the most famous, of the three Corpus men who have been Archbishops of Canterbury. He continued his benefactions to his old College, above all in his superb additions to its library. Many of the books he gave had been lovingly collected from the dispersed remnants of the great monastic libraries.

By the time of Parker's death in 1575 the numbers at Corpus had risen, in a little over ten years, from thirty-two to over ninety; more than half of those now resident were pensioners.

The Master, and most of the Fellows, leaned more to the Puritan party than Parker would have done, and by the end of the century the standing of Corpus Christi College had somewhat declined. Its most notable Elizabethan alumni had been the playwrights Marlowe and Fletcher, and Thomas Cavendish the gentlemen navigator who was, after Drake, the first Englishman to sail round the world. Drake himself, one finds, was a contributor to the simple late Gothic chapel, with a Renaissance doorway and a library above it, which was built between 1579 and 1584.

Physical expansion was now much needed in a college whose fortunes revived from the time of James I and whose numbers reached the new high level of one hundred and fifty-six in 1628. In the Mastership, from 1618 to 1626, of Dr Samuel Walsall there were some thoughts of building a new court, a project several times discussed in the next two hundred years before the work was actually done.

Though some of its Fellows were ejected by the parliamentary régime, Corpus had a less harrowing time under the Commonwealth than most others in Cambridge. In 1643 the Fellows went on leave of absence, and as much of the college plate was temporarily distributed among them, Corpus is still unusually rich in medieval silver. Dr Love, its Master from 1632 till 1661, kept on good terms with the country's new rulers. He was the only head of a Cambridge college not thrown out of his post in the Cromwellian period; at the Restoration he became Dean of Ely.

The Restoration period gave Benet College (as it was still called) a period of recovery and prosperity. Loggan's view shows that in 1688 its buildings remained unextended. Physical improvements, both then and in the coming century were confined to such things as the panelling and refurnishing of college rooms. Thomas Tenison, a Corpus man and Dr. Love's son-in-law, in 1694 became Archbishop of Canterbury, while the third primate from the college was Thomas Herring who got a Fellowship in 1716. Antiquarian studies were prominent at Corpus in Georgian days, and the college was remarkable, for that time, in the possession of a private laboratory.

In the eighteenth century two sets of plans were got out for a large new court in a simple classical style. Both of these courts were planned to open out into Trumpington Street, and James Essex's design of 1773 provided for the sweeping away of the picturesque Old Court. But nothing was done before 1822, and then in the 1820s the Perpendicular Gothic new court by Wilkins was successfully built. The bulk of the Old Court was kept and still survives. The building of the new court more than doubled the rooms in the college, gave Corpus a new chapel and provided a proper library for the housing of its splendid books.

Dr Lamb, the Master who built the new court, was a Whig of progressive views; at the end of his régime the undergraduate numbers at Corpus were the third largest in Cambridge. But for most of the Victorian period Corpus settled down as a small, conservative, strongly Evangelical College. Most of its graduates became Anglican clergymen, many of them serving in the mission field. Its large amount of new accommodation for a time kept Corpus's numbers high, but by 1900 it was again, as it has since remained, one of Cambridge's smallest colleges. Dr Perowne, who became Master in 1879, strongly opposed University and college reform, and one gets the impression, by the end of his long spell of office, of a somewhat stagnant society.

The present century has seen great changes in Corpus, and in its standing among Cambridge colleges. From about 1906 there came a remarkable transformation. The range of subjects studied was greatly widened, and new talent came, from other colleges, to the Corpus high table. While the college remained a centre of political conservatism its predominant churchmanship veered from strict Evangelical to moderate Anglo-Catholic. Dr Pearce, the college's Master who left to become Bishop of Derby, Sir Edwyn Hoskyns the prominent theologian, Sir Kenneth Pickthorn, historian and M.P., and Sir Will Spens, the college's first scientist Master were among those who best symbolised the new state of affairs. After inevitable upheavals in the first World War Corpus settled down to the college one knew between the wars. It was agreeably small, so that Corpus men dined at a single sitting, could know one another, and mostly lived in college. Its academic distinction was considerable, with modern languages and natural sciences the leading subjects.

In the second World War, Sir Will Spens was made Regional Commissioner for the Eastern Region, and it was from the buildings of Corpus that much of the work of the regional branches of Government departments was carried out.

Since the years just after 1945 Corpus has gone back to its policy of remaining a small college, and to the socially admirable practice, each evening, of a single sitting in the Hall. An interesting piece of structural renovation has been the total replacement, in stone less perishable than clunch, of the rectangular oriel in the old hall, itself a replacement, some time later than Loggan's print of 1688, of the semipolygonal fourteenth-century oriel whose original mullions had, by Loggan's time, been replaced by a simpler Elizabethan window pattern.

The undergraduates of Corpus now number about 200, and while no major change has occurred in the balance of subjects studied, natural sciences are now at the top. Mathematics, seldom read in Corpus before 1939, hold second place, and classics are stronger than in most other colleges.

As elsewhere, post-graduate residents have greatly increased. For their benefit, and to attract more of them, Corpus launched out, in a pioneering way, on its most notable social and architectural new venture. Since early last century the college has owned land, beyond Grange Road, which once formed part of the unenclosed 'Cambridge Field'. In 1878–80 the poet and educationist F. W. H. Myers built a house on a large part of this ground, naming it 'Leckhampton' after the village near Cheltenham where he had been a day boy at the College. The style of the house was supposed, in its rendering of red brick and not in stone, to recall the 'Cotswold' tradition of Gloucestershire. Having bought the balance of the lease the college has put this beautifully secluded property to imaginative use.

The old house, some nearby houses owned by Corpus, and the new Sir George Thomson building unite to give living accommodation and a common-room to six Fellows and some fifty married and unmarried research graduates; a fine new dining room has more recently been added. The group of buildings remains an integral part of the college, and Corpus now gives living space to three-quarters of its post-graduates. The new building, by Mr Philip Dowson and arranged in two main blocks connected by a 'service' section, is among the most admired, and admirable, of Cambridge's many new works of modern architecture. The Leckhampton complex well proves the vitality, after seven centuries of history, of the college system.

BUCKINGHAM

ONCE Corpus Christi College had got started on its career the first great surge of College founding in Cambridge came to an end. Nearly ninety years were to pass before the town saw the endowment, and the first building operations, on any College which survives with its original name. By then, moreover, an important development at Oxford had set out new standards of formal, systematic planning in the lay-out and building of academic Colleges.

But before one deals with the early schemes for King's, and with New College at Oxford which the royal founder of Eton and King's used for a model, another Cambridge College calls for attention. It no longer exists under its earlier name, or with the special character which it first possessed. But in a book which has covered the extinct Colleges of King's Hall and Michaelhouse one must also record the story of Buckingham College, a foundation of the fifteenth century whose buildings survive nearly intact as a main element, just North of the Great Bridge, of the still existing College which succeeded it.

Though most of the medieval students at Oxford and Cambridge came from the ranks of the secular, or non-monastic clergy, the monastic orders were not indifferent to the advantages, for some at least of their monks, of the higher studies pursued at the Universities. I have mentioned the hostel, for Benedictine student monks from Ely, which once stood on part of the site of Trinity Hall, and I have pointed out, in the section of this book which deals with Gonville and Caius College, how young monks from East Anglian Benedictine monasteries lodged in Gonville Hall. But more formal arrangements, under fuller monastic control, were also made, both at Oxford and Cambridge, for the accommodation and disciplined life of student monks. Monastic Colleges were started, and the chapels of those

Colleges gave facilities for the recitation of the choir offices which are the distinguishing element of monastic worship. The process went further at Oxford, and the buildings of its four monastic Colleges were incorporated, and in part remain, as elements in later Colleges. Canterbury College, founded by an Archbishop of Canterbury for Benedictine students, became part of Christ Church, its medieval buildings being replaced at the end of the eighteenth century. Some buildings of Durham College survive in the mid-Tudor College of Trinity. The attractive little houses of Gloucester College, which once lodged monastic students from various abbeys, are now a charming part of Worcester College. Even the secluded and contemplative Cistercians had their Oxford house of studies in St Bernard's College; its site, and some of its buildings, were reused in the 1550s by the new foundation of St John's. One gets the impression that educational work, of a type that needed graduate monks for its proper performance, may have been more important, in some abbeys, than some have supposed. This educational requirement is certainly the reason, nowadays, for the Benedictine houses of studies maintained, both at Oxford and Cambridge, by such abbeys as Ampleforth and Downside.

One Cambridge equivalent to the monastic Colleges at Oxford was that of St Edmund, built on a site across the road from Peterhouse, which later became that of Addenbrooke's Hospital. St Edmund's was established, as early as 1290–91, for Gilbertine canons of the order founded by St Gilbert of Sempringham. Until the dissolution it fulfilled its function, providing lodging and worshipping facilities for those members of the Order (almost wholly based on the eastern counties) who came to Cambridge for their higher studies. Then in the fifteenth century the Benedictines set up their Cambridge equivalent to their Order's three houses of studies at Oxford.

The Benedictine student monks at Cambridge had lived not in any monastic College but in academic hostels or in lodgings in the town. Their monastic discipline was apt to be weakened by such living conditions. The situation of those in lodgings was, after all, the very one which had, in the University's early days, caused the organisation of hostels and the foundation of Colleges. In 1423 the Prior who superintended these student monks suggested that a hostel should be started specially for them, and in 1426 the General Chapter of the English Benedictines, assembling that year at Northampton, complained of the existing state of affairs. In another two years some remedial action was taken. For Abbot Litlyngton of Croyland was granted leave to buy two houses, across the river and thus comparatively secluded from the main part of Cambridge, which become the first nucleus of a small monastic College.

The student monks who lived in the new 'Croyland' College came from other monasteries as well as that which had taken the new initiative. Ely, Ramsey, and Walden were among those which sent their members to reside there. But the ownership of the College seems to have remained with Croyland, and it was the abbot of that great Fenland monastery who was mainly responsible for any building work that was carried out. Abbot John de Wisbech, who succeeded Litlyngton, built much of what is now the Old Court of Magdalene College. The arms of the abbeys, which appear over some of Magdalene's staircase archways, were painted much later, and one need not suppose that those particular staircases were built to house monks from the abbeys whose heraldry so pleasantly decorates them. The buildings themselves, like those of Queens' which had been put up some thirty years earlier, are of clunch attractively faced with brick. A chapel, still that of Magdalene but much altered in the eighteenth century and since, was among the buildings finished about 1480. Soon after that time this Cambridge Benedictine College attracted the interest of the noble benefactors who came to give it their name.

The family, whose ducal title became that of the Benedictine College in Cambridge, was among the highest in the land. Henry Stafford, second Duke of Buckingham, was directly descended, on his mother's side, from Thomas of Woodstock, Duke of Gloucester, the youngest son of Edward III. His wife Catherine was a sister of Queen Elizabeth Woodville. He had powerfully helped Richard III to the throne. But he soon rebelled against the new king, unsuccessfully as it proved, and was executed in 1483. By then he had been a benefactor of Croyland Abbey, and he may even have started the building work on its dependency in Cambridge. His gifts to the monastic house of studies seem, in any case, to have been substantial, for by the year of his fall the Benedictine house of studies in Cambridge was known as Buckingham College. Under Henry VII, and early in the reign of his son, it continued its educational work. By the beginning of Henry VIII's reign Edward Stafford, the third Duke of Buckingham, had reached full manhood and was soon in the full, ostentatious flight of the dangerously ambitious career which, in 1521, brought him to the scaffold. He it was who built the simple, early Tudor hall of Buckingham College, a plain, workmanlike building in no way equalling the splendour of the Duke's castle at Thornbury in Gloucestershire, commenced in the style of the Court masons who worked on King's chapel at Cambridge, but left incomplete at his death.

In the early years of the sixteenth century some lay students, as well as student monks, were being taken at Buckingham College. This may have been due to a lack of numbers coming forward from the Benedictine monasteries. It certainly meant that, should monasticism in England pass away (as it soon did for nearly three centuries) one could still foresee a future for such a group of collegiate buildings. Then, in 1539, came the dissolution of the greater monasteries, with Croyland among them. This meant that Buckingham College, as an item of monastic property, fell to the Crown, thus coming under the control of the Court of Augmentations which handled the profitable disposal of almost a third of the land in England. It was a high official in that office who was, in part, responsible for the academic future of the little court, not yet complete along all of its four sides, but containing the main elements of a College, which had housed the student Benedictines of Buckingham College. The founding of Magdalene in 1542 had close links, through the person of its main instigator's chief associate in the work, with the starting, from a similar background and in Mary I's reign, of a well-known College at Oxford.

BUCKINGHAM (*opposite*). Monastic staircase, fifteenth century; the later arms are those of Walden Abbey

KING'S

THE second half of the fourteenth century was a fallow time for the founding of new colleges in Cambridge. But at Oxford, in the 1380s, the ordered, systematic splendour of the great foundation of New College was an important influence for the future both in Oxford itself and in the sister University. For a time, however, the University of Oxford lay under suspicion of Lollardy. So when the devout and highly orthodox monarchs of the House of Lancaster thought of new academic colleges they preferred Cambridge as the scene of their benefactions. Henry IV is said to have had some such Cambridge foundation in mind. It was, however, his young grandson who enlarged and glorified the idea, formed in the mind of a person of less than royal blood, for a new college.

The monastic college founded by Croyland Abbey was an establishment unlike those whose aim was the higher education of secular clergy. When the time came to start again with the foundation of colleges on the more normal pattern a man already very prominent in the University of Cambridge was the person whose notions made him a successor of such men as Bishops Balsham and Bateman, Hervey de Stanton, and Edmund Gonville. The man who seems to have had the idea which bore fruit in the royal foundation of King's College was John Langton, Master of Pembroke Hall, Chancellor of the University, and for a few days before his death in 1447 the Bishop of St David's. As Master of Pembroke he had obtained for his college the help and favour of the young King Henry VI, and he had been able to swell Pembroke's income by the method which duly provided most of the endowment of Eton and King's. He persuaded the king to become the founder of the modest college he himself had in mind. In 1440, when he must first have discussed his project with Henry, he could hardly have

KING'S (*opposite*). The Chapel, western end

foreseen how vastly the foundation was to be swollen beyond the rector and twelve scholars first envisaged for it.

The site first chosen for King's lay between Clare and the Old Schools. It was somewhat cramped, even for the modest numbers originally proposed. It was blocked, on its eastern side, by the still surviving buildings of the Schools. Unless these had been obtained and cleared away a four-sided court would always have been impossible, and the site allowed no room for expansion. As it was, the hall built to serve the inmates of the Old Court of King's curiously overlapped the northern range of the schools. But the court gained in impressiveness, and in the living space which it provided, by being built from the first with the innovating number of three storeys. Its splendid gateway was never finished, for by the time of its commencement other plans were afoot for the future of King's. The College was being enlarged, and endowed, in such a way that it almost resembled a University on its own with a status in Cambridge which was amazingly privileged, and not, in the long run to its own advantage.

By 1443 the King had decided to link his Cambridge College with the large foundation he had already made, for grammar scholars of a more tender age, at Eton close to Windsor. As Eton was due to turn out large numbers of young scholars his Cambridge college had also to be large. Henry's new scheme, for no less than seventy Fellows as well as several chaplains, lay clerks, and choristers, made King's a far larger foundation than any others already existing in Cambridge. To the minds of Henry VI and his advisers it seemed obvious that a new site, far more spacious than the court already started, would be needed to hold the domestic buildings, and the enormous chapel, which the king now had in mind. What he could not foresee was that the members of his augmented foundation would long have to make do with the incomplete buildings of the original court.

Bold steps were taken to endow the enlarged college and to obtain ground for the buildings now projected. The college's revenues, like those of Eton, were largely found by diverting endowments which had once belonged to the numerous monasteries in France which had dependent priories, or other estates, in various parts of England. Earlier in the century, when the war with France was at its height, these possessions had been made over to the Crown. Their revenues were gradually applied, within England itself, to other religious institutions. New College and other Oxford colleges, Pembroke Hall at Cambridge, and Eton and King's all benefited in this way. In addition, the ample revenues of the Duchy of Lancaster provided much of the capital sum required for the early building work which was done on King's chapel. To house the college, with its chapel nearly three hundred feet long and with its complete buildings which were obviously inspired by those of New College at Oxford, the King bought a large area between High Street (now King's Parade) and the river. The drastic clearance of this site, once filled by streets, houses, and some of Cambridge's riverside wharves, meant the end of most of Cambridge as a riverside town. The parish church of St John Zachary (i.e. the Baptist) was pulled down, and its living was in time merged with that of St Edward's. The small Grammar College of God's House, lately founded on a site close to the western end of the great new chapel, was moved to a site, near Barnwell Gate, which made it the first of Cambridge's eastern belt of colleges.

The chapel was the first building of the expanded royal foundation to be taken in hand, and the King laid its foundation stone in 1446. It must have been foreseen that so vast a building would not be usable for many years, so that a temporary chapel, of fair size, was put up in the space between the larger chapel and the Old Court.

Meanwhile, King's College had been so organised as to put it in a highly special position in the University of Cambridge. It was made exempt from the jurisdiction of the University's Chancellor, and also from that of the Bishop of Ely in whose diocese Cambridge lay. The Bishop of Lincoln, whose vast diocese included Buckinghamshire and who was already the Visitor of Eton College, was given the same position in relation to King's. In due course one also had the anomaly that Kingsmen were exempt, for the purposes of gaining their B.A. degrees, from University examinations. In addition, one saw Henry VI's highhanded act whereby Cambridge's other royal college of King's Hall was for the rest of his reign made subject to King's. Such a privileged state no doubt seemed appropriate for a foundation which was both sumptous and under royal direction; as things turned out it long proved a mixed blessing both to the University as a whole and to King's College itself.

The King's full scheme for his college, with its large, systematically designed court, and with its cloistered cemetery overlooked, as at New College, Oxford, by a tall belfry, could have been completed had the House of Lancaster prospered for some four or five decades after 1446. But the project was severely frustrated by the Wars of the Roses, and by the political fall of Henry VI. Only part of the eastern half of the chapel had been built by 1461; hardly anything had been done on the domestic ranges which were to surround the spacious court whose more immediate legacy to Cambridge seems to have been seen in the idea of such spaciousness actually realised, next century, in Trinity and St John's.

The Yorkists took away nearly half of the revenues of this eminently

Lancastrian College. At the same time, more justifiably, they gave back its independence to the no less royal foundation of King's Hall, thus opening the way to the eventual foundation of Trinity.

By 1465 the Fellows and scholars of King's numbered no more than twenty-three; it was nearly a century before they were back to the full number of seventy. The College's activities were restricted within the confines of the Old Court, and in the temporary chapel. The unfinished bulk of the greater chapel's choir loomed up to the South, a standing reminder of frustrated hopes. Yet under Edward IV, and still more under Richard III, a good deal of work was done on the chapel. But under Henry VII the tightness of the royal finances stopped work for over twenty years. Only towards the end of his reign, and urged on by Lady Margaret, his mother, did the first Tudor monarch make funds available for what was, at last to prove the final building phase of the chapel's fabric. Now, moreover, more elaborate designs were used than the comparatively simple ones worked on by Henry VI's masons. It seems that a fan vault, not the rib vault at first allowed for, had already been decided upon, and John Wastell's actual fan vault made a dramatic elaboration on what had first been envisaged. The antechapel, moreover, was made the scene for a stupendous and vaunting political display of Tudor badges and heraldry. The masonary and timber fabric of the chapel was complete by the end of 1515. The windows and the Renaissance screen which is, if anything, an even greater glory than the glass, were installed by the end of 1536, ninety years exactly after Henry VI had laid the foundation stone. Some of the chantry chapels between the buttresses were, however, already in use.

The Reformation period had come by the time that King's chapel was finished. The initials of Henry VIII, and of Anne Boleyn as his queen, are carved on the screen and remind us of the changes which were afoot when that superb piece of church furniture was set up. A few years earlier John Frith, a friend of the Bible translator William Tyndale, and one of the Cambridge scholars who had helped to staff Christ Church at Oxford, had been the first Kingsman to die for his religious opinions. Most of those who came to King's from Eton studied theology, though a few civil and canon lawyers, and fewer medics and astrologers, were also among them.

Classical studies were well established in King's quite early in the college's history, and the keen Protestant Sir John Cheke, who was Provost under Edward VI, would have found King's a congenial home for one who had been the University's first Regius Professor of Greek.

The college's main trouble, as it entered the second half of the sixteenth century, lay in the serious gap, in its living quarters, between the founder's

intentions and the stone-built reality. It was a good point that its foundationers had now climbed back to the number allowed for in the statutes
given by Henry VI. One also noticed that King's, like other colleges in
Cambridge, now had its entry of fellow commoners and poor scholars. But
non-foundationers, who meant so much for the coming development of
other Cambridge colleges, could not help being few in a College which had
still to cram over seventy members into a court planned for a rector and
twelve Fellows.

One might almost say, in a version of the joking rhyme made up about
Wolsey's efforts to get his Cardinal College started at Oxford, that whereas
Wolsey had planned a college but had himself built no more than an eating
house (i.e. the hall of Christ Church), the foundation commenced at
Cambridge by Henry VI had not much more than the superb House of God
in whose dim space the entire membership of King's College seemed almost
lost beneath the scarce-perceived compartments of John Wastell's noble fan
vault.

The Elizabethan Age saw King's College in a phase of prosperity and
varied innovation. No large increase was possible in the number of its
members, but a few pensioners were entered at this time and the old St
Austin's Hostel (near the site of the present hall) was taken over, enlarged,
and converted to house them. Pensioners did not, however, remain a
continuous element among Kingsmen, and for their revival one had to await
the second half of the nineteenth century.

Some few years passed before the Anglican settlement of England's
religious affairs was wholly accepted in King's. Provost Baker, who had
to resign in 1569, was a 'crypto Catholic' whose concealment of his real
religious sympathies wore somewhat thin. Like Dr Caius in his augmented
college, Baker kept hidden in his lodge, anent their possible re-use, stocks
of missals, crosses, copes, and pyxes. It was Roger Goad, Baker's successor
and the Provost of King's for more than forty years, who set the college
more firmly on the Protestant path. He himself was a zealous Protestant,
who also reorganised the college library and started a new series of college
lectures. The completed chapel was now accepted as one of the main sights
of Cambridge. When, in 1564, Elizabeth I came to Cambridge, she visited
the building, both to attend services and to watch the performance of a
Latin play by Plautus set in front of the highly classical, and in many
ways appropriate, background of the screen.

The last years of Goad's provostship were filled with much contention
between him and the Fellows. But the reputation of King's still stood high,
and the earliest years of the seventeenth century were also those when the

outstanding musical traditions of King's took firm root. In 1606, about the time when a new organ was set up, and when the first really excellent choral services were held, John Tomkins was made organist.

The services were increasingly attended by townspeople from outside the college, and King's Chapel (to its later advantage) seemed more and more to be the possession not of a single college but of all Cambridge. The early years of the seventeenth century were also a time when non-foundationers were more numerous in King's than they had been in previous years. In 1623 the college had as many as thirty-seven undergraduates who were not on its foundation. But the increase was not maintained, the inhibiting factor being the lack of accommodation in the Old Court. Under Charles I, when the Stuart régime seemed stable and secure, the Fellows had it in mind to complete the college's buildings along the lines projected by Henry VI. But nothing had been done by the beginning of the Civil War, and there then came a time when all that Kingsmen could hope for was the preservation of the glories they already possessed.

In the Civil War, and under the Commonwealth, King's shared the experiences of most other colleges whose sympathies had been staunchly Royalist. Provost Collins lost his post, and it was the great good fortune of King's that his successor was the moderate, conciliatory Benjamin Whichcote. Like many others who obtained important Cambridge posts at this time, Whichcote was an Emmanuel man.

He was a leading figure among the Cambridge Platonists, and he did what he could, for Fellows of King's who were ejected or who actually served in the Royalist armies, to temper the distresses inevitable, for those on the losing side, in a time of Puritan supremacy. What seems remarkable is that the windows of the chapel were spared at a time when William Dowsing, under Parliament orders, was causing much artistic havoc elsewhere in Cambridge and in churches up and down the eastern counties. Whichcote was a friend of Cromwell and he, like Milton who clearly admired the chapel at King's, could have influenced him to leave the glass untouched. But at the time of Dowsing's activities Whichcote was still far away, in Somerset, in his Emmanuel living of North Cadbury. So factors of a more generally political kind may have lain behind the happy survival of the windows; the screen and the stallwork were less obviously controversial in their decoration and could in any case have been expected to survive. Dowsing's attacks were largely made on 'Laudian' furnishings such as those in the chapel at Peterhouse (although even there he left the East Window unbroken), and one also had the practical point that the reglazing of the windows in King's with clear glass would have been an enormous task.

King's Chapel, moreover, was by now held in high esteem among the townsmen as well as in the University. A politic desire to conciliate local feeling may have had something to do with the sparing of the windows in King's despite Dowsing's ominous note that steps were to be taken over the thousand 'superstitious pictures', which seem likely to have included the windows that he found in the chapel.

Life at King's, with Whichcote as Provost, continued placidly enough under the Parliamentary régime, and twenty-nine scholars were admitted in the years 1649–51. But Whichcote himself, though much respected, lost his headship of King's at the Restoration, and the last decades of the seventeenth century ushered in a period of distinct decline. It was probably a misfortune for the college when in 1689 the proposal to have Sir Isaac Newton as Provost was rejected; King's certainly lost its chance of the most distinguished Provost it could have had among all those who have ruled it. A little earlier, in 1686, Lord Dartmouth had urged the college to collect money for the proper completion of its buildings. But no more was done in those years than the erection, not far from the line of the present King's Parade, of a building which contained a choristers' school and some accommodation for Fellow Commoners and sizars.

Not until the next century was well under way was a start made with the desperately overdue task of adding to the college's more important buildings. By then, moreover, King's was deep in the grip of a long stagnation caused by its lack of living space, its isolation from the rest of the University, and its excessive recruitment from one particular school.

The movement to build worthily on the site Henry VI had bought for the domestic portions of his college got seriously under way in the early years of the eighteenth century. Provost Adams commissioned Hawksmoor to get out some dignified designs, in the restrained Baroque of which that architect was so fine a master. The Provost intended that the cemetery and the bell tower mentioned in the founder's 'Will' should also be built. But nothing was done to realise Hawksmoor's scheme, and when in the 1720s a start was made with 'The New College' the chosen architect was James Gibbs. The present Gibbs Building was taken in hand in 1724. But the exhaustion of the available money meant that it was finished as one block only of three that were projected. The hall block, across the court from the chapel, was also to have contained a new Provost's Lodge, and one assumes that its completion would have meant the pulling down of the rambling, inconvenient building, east of the chapel, which had long housed the head of the college. It seems, moreover, that had all the proposed new blocks been finished the Old Court would have been given up. As the Gibbs Building which actually exists, and its opposite number across the court, would only between them have contained sets for forty-eight Fellows it appears that no more Kingsmen were to be housed in the new college than those allowed for by Henry VI's foundation. There seems to have been no desire to expand beyond those limits or to increase the college's junior members by admissions from new sources.

The Gibbs Building, when finished in 1730, stood alone without its twin block, and without the splendid porticoed hall Gibbs had designed. Its rooms were palatial and one hears that they were unpopular with those who preferred to be closer to the hall, and to the social and domestic facilities, of the Old Court. One can imagine, when one thinks of the short stroll round the west end of the chapel, what these leisured dons of the Augustan age would have thought of the distance to college from the Garden Hostel of King's or the Harvey Court of Caius.

The main trouble with King's in the eighteenth century, and indeed until the 1850s, was that it was an inward-looking, restricted society of Fellows and scholars who all came to it from Eton. It had become the custom, though without real warrant from the founder's statutes, that Kingsmen should get their B.A. degrees without taking University examinations.

The college had become intensely and predominantly classical, and Kingsmen shrank from what they felt to be the tyranny of the mathematics which had, in those days, to be faced by the Cambridge men who qualified in classics. King's was not, in the Georgian period, anything like so distinguished an academic college as it is today. Sir Robert Walpole stood out as its most eminent alumnus. Walpole's son, Horace, was also at King's, but does not seem to have gained the stimulus that a man of his aesthetic temperament would get there now.

The future Lord Chancellor Camden was a Kingsman, and the dilettante poetic satirist, Christopher Anstey, was a Fellow. Another Fellow was Sir William Draper, a man of literary interests who forsook Cambridge for the Army, and fought with distinction in India. When in 1762 he commanded the troops who took Manila he sent some Spanish colours from the capital of the Philippines to be hung on each side of the sanctuary in King's Chapel.

The first half of the nineteenth century was doubly important for King's. Between 1824 and 1828 the founder's plans for college buildings were in essence completed, though with a screen, not an accommodation block, on the side of King's Parade. The architect, in the Tudor Gothic which he now favoured, was William Wilkins, and soon after 1828 the Old

Court was sold to the University. By this time the process of academic reform was starting both at Eton and King's, and the college, though not yet the University itself, held examinations for Kingsmen who were qualifying for their B.A. degrees. Several members of the college now felt that Kingsmen should submit themselves to the University examiners, but this change was blocked, all through his provostship, by George Thackeray, a relative of the novelist (who was a Trinity man) and a member of a family well known both at King's and Eton.

Soon after Thackeray died in 1850 it was quickly and easily agreed that King's should give up its exemption from the University's degree examinations. Other changes followed, among them the creation of open (i.e. non-Etonian) Fellowships and the admission, in 1865, of exhibitioners and pensioners. Some two decades passed before these reforms became fully effective and the first non-Etonian Fellow (the father of the poet Rupert Brooke) was not seen in King's until 1873.

But these mid-Victorian changes led to increases both in the college's undergraduate numbers (seventy-one 1880 as against twenty-one only twelve years earlier) and in the extent of the college's living quarters. They also opened the way to the varied, progressive brilliance one now associates with this richly endowed college of royal foundation. By 1879, King's flourished so greatly that it proposed, unsuccessfully, an amalgamation with its southerly, and then languishing, neighbour St Catharine's.

By the beginning of this century King's had settled down to a modern career which was worthily reflected in its position in the University as a whole. It was, overwhelmingly an arts college, with all its undergraduates reading for honours, and with Kingsmen drawn from all the sources whence Cambridge men were then apt to be recruited. The splendid musical standards of the chapel were by now well established, and to meet its rising numbers the college extended its buildings, somewhat scrappily and leaving intact the great lawn first laid out in 1772, along the southernmost stretch of its territory. Lowes Dickinson, Montagu James, J. C. Clapham and Maynard Keynes were among the most brilliant Kingsmen of this time. Another was the young Rupert Brooke.

The inter-war life of King's confirmed the impressions of the century's earlier years, and the college's almost complete concentration on arts subjects meant that aesthetes and literary intellectuals were more prominent among its members than in other colleges. Choral scholars now wholly replaced the lay clerks who had long sung in the chapel while the chapel and its music gained still greater fame from broadcasts at Christmas and at other times. A reverse aspect of the college's supreme glory has been the heavy financial burden of its maintenance, a burden not lightened by the dangerous and (to King's) costly activities of the Cambridge night-climbers.

It was as well for King's that its revenues were stabilised and increased by the financial abilities of Maynard Keynes, whose brilliant bursarship was more important for the college than the provostships of most of the men who had been its heads. Financial prosperity has made it possible for King's to have many more Fellows, in relationship to its undergraduates, than most other colleges in Cambridge. It has also been possible, before 1939 and still more since 1945, to offer unusually many research student-ships for post-graduate work. Contrary to the belief of many outsiders, King's has remained a small college. Before the late war its undergraduates only numbered about two hundred. They have now, after an inevitably steep rise soon after 1945, been kept at about two hundred and eighty. King's is still, in the main, an arts college. But the proportion of Kingsmen reading science is now over a sixth of the whole—a far higher proportion than in the 1930s.

For some time after 1945 its building expansion was confined to the Garden and Market Hostels; much money had also to be spent on the stone-work of the chapel and on the cleaning, rearrangement and replacement of the glass which had been taken out of its windows for safety in wartime.

Modern work, of great significance and complete by the end of 1970, is found in the development which King's and St Catharine's, in a pioneering act of intercollegiate co-operation, jointly carried out on the ground between their older buildings. King's Lane, once known as Plott and Nuts Lane, has been realigned, and the new buildings, by Sir James Cubitt and Partners, straddle the boundary between the two Colleges. The section of the new building complex which belongs to King's contains accommodation for about 90 undergraduates. The other buildings—with their quiet enclosure and their vista, past a fountain and gates shut at night, over the lane and so into St Catharine's—contain a few Fellows' sets, a research centre, and the Keynes Hall which is used for such events as lectures and musical recitals. In addition, the College kitchens have been so reorganised that all under-graduate meals, though taken in the main hall, are served on the cafeteria system.

The most important recent institutional change in King's has been the arrival, at the beginning of the academic year of 1972–73, of the College's first female undergraduates; a woman tutor had been appointed before they came up. Thirty-seven women have thus entered King's, none of them being open scholars; there was heavy competition for the places. They are housed, differently from the system adopted in Clare, on various and dispersed staircases.

A final point concerns the chapel which will always be the supreme glory of King's. The year 1972 saw the publication of Mr Hilary Wayment's splendid monogram on the windows; it should long remain a definitive authority on an absorbing subject.

QUEENS'

ONCE the great foundation of King's had been set on its way by the energetic generosity of a reigning sovereign it was logical enough that the wife of that king should have her title associated with a new college in Cambridge. But whereas, at King's Henry VI was himself the main founder, though not the originator of the idea, at Queens' one finds that his consort's help was more nominal, and that the essential work was done by someone else.

The real founder of Queens' was a secular priest, Andrew Doket who was rector of St Botolph's Church and who was also the Principal of the large, college-like Hostel of St Bernard whose ambitious buildings stood, not far to the North of his church, on the site later covered by the New Court of Corpus. By the mid-1440s the founding of colleges had again got under way in Cambridge, and it must have been soon after the commencement of building work on King's that Doket, along with some of his well-to-do parishioners, formed the scheme of founding a small college of his own.

The origins of Queens', like those of Corpus, lie in the town life of medieval Cambridge. Late in 1446 (no doubt after some months at least of preliminary planning) Doket obtained, from Henry VI, a charter of foundation for a small college, like his hostel named after St Bernard. It was to stand on a site across Trumpington Street from St Bernard's Hostel, between that street and Milne Street whose remaining fragment is now Queens' Lane. It was to consist of no more than a President and four Fellows. Doket himself seems not to have been a man of any great wealth. But he got handsome benefactions from various neighbouring townsmen. Richard Andrew, a rich burgess and a parishioner of St Botolph's, was among them; he later appeared as an important benefactor to Doket's larger, and reorganised, foundation.

But St Bernard's College was never built on the site first chosen by Doket; had it arisen there it would have had a cramped, unexpandable site, and St Catharine's would have been even more congested than it is. In 1447 Doket obtained a site, across Milne Street and between that street and the river, better than that he had first bought, and which Queens' long kept. One has, however, to remember that as the Carmelite Friary still lay to the north, his college at first had much less ground than Queens' as we now admire it. Soon after he had made plans to build on this more westerly site, Doket obtained for his foundation the prestige of a royal appellation. Queen Margaret of Anjou, the eighteen-year-old wife of the founder of King's, was persuaded to be called the foundress of the re-sited St Bernard's.

A new charter formally recognised the position whereby the new college became the Queen's (one queen only) College of Saints Margaret and Bernard. This Charter dates from April 15th, 1448. On that same day the Queen's chamberlain laid the chapel's foundation stone, and Queen Margaret's arms became, and within a green bordure remain, those of Doket's College; thanks to the family background of Queen Margaret they form the most complex coat borne by any Cambridge College. The Queen's interest does not, however, seem to have included a strong financial side, and Doket's foundation provided for no more than the President and four Fellows of two years before.

Doket was able, in the meantime, to carry on with the building of his college's single court. From the time of its first construction Queens' possessed all the elements—hall, chapel, library, living accommodation and a fine gate tower containing its muniment room—which one had, by now, come to associate with an academic college. Reginald Ely was the designer, and Queens' was the first Cambridge College to have all its buildings put up in brick-faced clunch. By about 1454 the first court of the college was finished, standing as a remarkably compact and complete piece of collegiate planning on a modest scale.

By the mid 1460s the House of Lancaster had fallen and Queen Margaret was soon in exile. But Doket himself seems not to have been politically compromised and he succeeded, by 1465, in obtaining for his college the patronage of the new Queen, Elizabeth Woodville, herself of a Lancastrian family and a friend of Queen Margaret. It was thus that the apostrophe in the name of his college got moved to the end of the titular word. In 1475, when the first statutes came into force, the Fellows of Queens' had risen from four to twelve and the block of buildings along the riverside had probably been built.

Another Yorkist benefactor now appeared in the person of Richard,

Duke of Gloucester, and when he became King Richard III he made extra grants. It was during his reign, in 1484, that Andrew Doket died. Unlike the founders of Peterhouse, Gonville Hall, and Trinity Hall, he had been spared for many years to see his college on its way to lasting usefulness and success; he must rank among the best, and most businesslike, of those who have founded colleges in Cambridge.

The fall of the last Yorkist king was a worse misfortune for Queens' than the collapse of its original Lancastrian patrons. For the grants made by Richard III were revoked under Henry VII: had the college kept them its income would have more than doubled.

Early in the sixteenth century Queens' was associated with two men of more national, and indeed international, fame than the Cambridge parish priest who had founded the college. From 1505 to 1508 John Fisher was its president. He had, in 1504, become Bishop of Rochester and Chancellor of the University and it seems that he found his headship of Queens' a convenient means of giving him a secure place of residence in Cambridge.

Then in 1510, while Fisher was still Chancellor and a man of great influence in Cambridge, the famous Renaissance scholar Erasmus came to the University for four years, residing in Queens'. Despite his complaints about Cambridge in general, and in particular about the beer and wine he could get there, he made some friends in Queens' and his residence there gave him good chances for lecturing, writing, and general study.

Not long after his sojourn in their college, Queens' men were involved in the controversies of the Reformation. Thomas Farman, the President, was among the 'White Horse' group of Reformers, but Queens' was not a college where the religious changes of those times seem to have caused much bitterness or strife. An important domestic event, coming late in Henry VIII's reign, was when Queens' greatly enlarged its site by taking most of the ground once occupied by the Carmelite Friary.

The next few years were comparatively uneventful and for a marked rise in its prosperity Queens' awaited a more settled period under Elizabeth I. Its total strength in 1564, including a few fee-paying 'pensioners', was sixty-five, in another nine years numbers were up to 122, with no fewer than 77 pensioners. The future Archbishop Whitgift was a pensioner at Queens' and apart from the notable figure of Sir Thomas Smith, a lawyer whose influence with Queen Catherine Parr was a help to the whole University, the Queens' men whose careers lay in the sixteenth century included some Bishops and other men who achieved reasonable eminence.

As in many other colleges, the early Stuart period saw a temporary peak in the fortunes of Queens', with the remarkably large membership of

230 in 1621; a new building had by then been erected to help house the influx.

Like all too many other Cambridge Colleges, Queens' declined badly in the eighteenth century; its complete membership, about 1750, was only around sixty. Its Fellows were not, however, deterred from altering and improving their buildings. The chapel was refurnished, the hall was ceiled and elegantly re-panelled and down by the river one sees how a start was made on a large block by James Essex which would, had it been finished, have caused the sad loss of all the late medieval riverside range. Late in the century some of the college's land across the Granta was used by Isaac Milner, who was Jacksonian Professor of Natural Philosophy and one of Queens' more notable Presidents, for the building of a small chemical laboratory. Later in the Georgian period the college's numbers again increased, and by the end of the Napoleonic War Queens' was Cambridge's fourth largest college. Its religious outlook was Low Church, while among its Fellows was George Cornelius Gorham, whose views on baptism caused trouble even at his ordination, and who was, many years later, a central figure in a great controversy on the same topic which severely troubled the Church of England. A quaint point about him is that in 1812 Gorham was the last Fellow of Queens' to preach a sermon endowed in 1593 (for delivery at Huntingdon) against the practice of witchcraft.

Later in the nineteenth century a good deal was done to renovate various buildings in Queens' and the site, across Queens' Lane, originally intended by Doket for his St Bernard's College, was sold to St Catharine's. The architect Bodley was employed both on renovations to the old chapel and on St Botolph's church whose patronage was (and is) held by Queens'. Then in the 1890s it was Bodley, along with his partner, Thomas Garner, who designed the new chapel which is one of Cambridge's better Victorian buildings. The college's endowed income was heavily hit by now as a result of the great agricultural depression which set in about 1879. But compensation came from the taking in of more pensioner undergraduates and more new buildings were needed to hold them.

Lastly one comes to the history, undramatic yet quietly progressive, of present-day Queens'. Finance has been a crucial and a limiting factor; it is not always realised in Cambridge that Queens', though an old and outstandingly beautiful college, is one of the most slenderly endowed. Its alumni, this century, have included Bishop Joost de Blank, Sir Leslie Rowan, and Prof Henry Chadwick, who was Regius Professor of Divinity at Oxford.

Just before the late war the new Fisher Building was a major expansion of the college on its ground across the river. More recently, and with much greater architectural distinction, the excellent block by Sir Basil Spence has made more of an enclosed court of the one-time Carmelite site and was financed by an appeal to Queens' men.

With more post-graduates than in former days, and with an under-graduate strength about four hundred, Queens' is now fourth or fifth, in point of numbers, among the colleges of Cambridge. Until lately its Fellows were fewer, in relation to its junior members, than in most other colleges. But eight were elected in 1965 and Queens' is trying to restrict its intake of undergraduates. As elsewhere in Cambridge the proportion of those reading sciences is higher than it was before 1939, while medicine and engineering are also strong among the present generation of Queens' men. But the college's second strongest subject is law, with history and economics well represented among those whose academic home makes Queens' a college of such outstanding 'touristic' appeal.

The leading factor in the most recent history of Queens' has been the starting, late in 1971, of the first phase of a new building complex, across the river from the original College, which will make it possible for all Queens' men to live in College, and which will also, as at Caius in the 1850s and very recently at St Catharine's, give Queens' a new, far larger hall to replace one which has served since the College's early days. The scheme makes up the most important building job now (early in 1973) under way in any Cambridge College, and its first phase is due for completion in 1974. The main structure is being financed by the Cripps Foundation, which has already greatly benefited two other Cambridge Colleges; the architects are the London firm of Powell and Moya. The Fellows' garden, across the river, has been given up to form part of the site and the buildings will, when all of them are complete, contain rooms for about 145 undergraduates and a few Fellows. There will also be a new sick bay, new Combination Rooms for senior members, post-graduates, and undergraduates and also, beneath a somewhat graceless and barnlike roof structure, a spacious new hall whose use as the College's main dining place will leave the hall of Doket's time available for special parties and small-scale dining. A new footbridge, from the new court to what was once the Carmelite area, will enable Queens' to share with St. John's the distinction, among the riverside Colleges of Cambridge, of having two bridges across the Granta.

ST CATHARINE'S

By the middle years of the fifteenth century thirteen colleges, including God's House and two monastic ones, had been founded in Cambridge. As most of these colleges were in the space between the High Street and the river, that part of the town, with several academic hostels as well as the endowed colleges, was becoming very full of various places of learning. There was, however, enough ground for the building of one more small college, but it was no surprise that Catharine Hall was the last college to occupy a *new* site in what was now an overwhelmingly academic sector of Cambridge. Only by the suppression of existing religious foundations could a new college (St John's) and the expansion of Queens' be fitted, in later years, between the river and the long, historic thoroughfare whose southern stretch is now known as Trumpington Street.

The founder of Catharine Hall was Robert Wodelarke, who was Provost of King's between 1452 and 1479. His time of office included the Lancastrian collapse and most of the Yorkists' rule. Though he founded his college not as Provost of King's but as a private venture, the disasters which befell the larger college, along with some losses of his own, delayed and diminished his more modest project.

He started his plans at least as early as 1459, and then for a college of a Master and ten Fellows (the latter to be on advanced studies in philosophy and theology) instead of the diminutive figure of three Fellows, in addition to the Master, with whom Catharine Hall actually opened in 1473. The site of the little college, in those days looking out on to Milne Street (now Queens' Lane), formed the nucleus of the expanded but still congested site with which the present college has still to be satisfied.

As at Corpus Christi, a strong 'chantry' purpose pervaded Wodelarke's

73

foundation, the Fellows being bound to celebrate requiem masses, and to recite other prayers, for the founder's soul. The small scale of the project as eventually carried out meant that Wodelarke, like Doket at Queens' across the street, but unlike the royal founder of the college over which he presided, lived to see Catharine Hall completed in accordance with the second, more modest plans enforced on him by the confused politics of his age.

From 1475, when a royal charter allowed Catharine Hall to hold property, the little college continued steadily on its modest career. In 1515 its Fellows, who had as companions a few Fellow Commoners, a Bible clerk, and some sizars who were both students and genteel servitors, were increased to six. The early years of the sixteenth century saw them receive some gifts for building work on their humble little court, whose ranges, whether timber-framed or of clunch, seem from the start to have been somewhat poorly built.

In 1535, when the *Valor Ecclesiasticus* gave figures for the incomes of the Oxford and Cambridge colleges, Catharine Hall still had the lowest endowment in Cambridge. A few years later the college's financial position was little better but it had, in the meantime, produced Masters for three other colleges.

Until the middle years of the sixteenth century Catharine Hall, like other colleges in their earliest days, was a society entirely made up of postgraduate scholars, absorbed in their studies and in the corporate worship which their founder's instructions bound them regularly to render. But from now onwards Catharine Hall became more and more of a teaching college with its junior members increasing in number and with extra subjects, such as law and medicine, added to the philosophy and theology already taught there.

The rest of the sixteenth century, and the first quarter of the one which followed, none the less made up a confused and difficult period for Catharine Hall, with disputes among the Fellows to offset increased numbers of undergraduate members. New buildings were needed, soon after 1610, to help house the increase, and then in the 1630s the college put up the recently demolished Gostlin building, of brick-faced clunch with mullioned windows, whose erection formed part of the college's complete rebuilding which took place in the seventeenth century.

By 1634, when the Puritan Richard Sibbes was Master, Catharine Hall had entered what proved to be an excellent period in its history, with good teaching given in the college and a valuable gift made to it in the form of the adjacent Bull Inn. Any further building work which the Fellows of Catharine Hall may have had in mind soon after 1634 was delayed and frustrated by the troubles of the Civil War. John Spurstow who became Master in 1650 when his Royalist predecessor was ejected, gave the college twenty-five years of prosperous rule.

Then, in 1675, John Eachard, already a successful tutor in the college, was elected its Master. For Catharine Hall, he became almost as much of a benefactor as Dr Caius had been for his college. After he died in 1697 the inscription on his memorial tablet in the new chapel fittingly called him *secundus . . . huius Romae Romulus.*

It was in Eachard's time that the steady replacement of the old buildings by a larger, most dignified brick and stone court in the Baroque idiom was actively taken in hand. The chapel had still to be built when Eachard died, and Catharine Hall never got the fourth block, on the Trumpington Street side of its court, which Loggan's engraving shows to have been planned. But Dr Eachard's energetic efforts to collect the needful money had their reward, and his Mastership was the time which gave us the main essence of the St Catharine's of today. Eachard also tried, without lasting success, to form special links between Catharine Hall and certain schools, including King Edward VI's at Birmingham.

The eighteenth century was a time of placid decline in Catharine Hall; about the middle of the century only some twenty-five undergraduates were in residence there. An important and more happy event was the large benefaction of Mrs Mary Ramsden, a Yorkshire lady whose great uncle, Robert Skerne, had earlier endowed some scholarships in the College. Mrs Ramsden's money made it possible to complete the court, three-sided and open onto Trumpington Street, which is still so attractive an element in the Cambridge scene. The new piece of building was meant to house the bye-Fellows (known as Skerne Fellows) and the scholars provided for under the new bequest. Earlier in the eighteenth century a Fellow of Catharine Hall was Dr John Addenbrooke, who was bursar in 1709 and who died in 1719, over forty years before work actually started in the famous hospital founded under his bequest.

The early years of the next century were an active and vigorous period in Catharine Hall, as indeed they were elsewhere in Cambridge. George Elwes Corrie, the Evangelical and staunchly conservative Fellow who was, for thirty-two years, a successful tutor in Catharine Hall went on, for another long spell until his death, aged ninety-two, to be Master of Jesus.

In 1847, when Dr Philpott, the Master of Catharine Hall, was Vice-Chancellor, Queen Victoria and the Prince Consort dined in the college during their visit to Cambridge, and in 1860 the college's title was changed to that of St Catharine's College. In the next year Dr Philpott left to become

Bishop of Worcester. There soon followed a sad and astonishing spell of ostracism and social decline, with few equivalents in the college histories either of Oxford or Cambridge.

There were two candidates for the vacant Mastership of St Catharine's. One of them, Charles Kirkby Robinson, secured the post by the addition of his own vote to those of some other Fellows. It was not unusual, in such elections, for candidates to vote for themselves; what seems to have been doubtful was whether or not Robinson and Jameson, the other contender, had agreed to vote for each other. Another probable source of the loser's eventual bitterness was that Robinson, only a few days after his election, got married; had he done so only a little earlier, before Philpott's Worcester appointment was known, he would have vacated his Fellowship and so disqualified himself.

Whatever his grievance, Jameson made it widely known, and a long pamphlet war ensued. The reputation of St Catharine's declined, and for the rest of the century the college was so shunned that the numbers and the quality of its undergraduates fell heavily. Things were not improved by Robinson's inordinately long, forty-eight year tenure of his Mastership. Yet there were in this period some St Catharine's men of real distinction; among them were Dr Forrest Browne, who became Bishop of Bristol, and G. G. Coulton, the great medieval scholar. Considerable building work, including a new Master's Lodge and the sad Gothicising of the hall, went on in the eight years which followed 1868, and in 1879 St Catharine's was still strong and proud enough to reject the suggested amalgamation with King's.

The slow revival of St Catharine's started soon after 1909, but its main process occurred in the years which followed the First World War. Resident Fellows and undergraduates alike increased and new buildings in imitation Baroque were put up on each side of the Trumpington Street entrance to the court. This was also a time when the athletic reputation of 'Cat's' particularly on the Rugby field, stood very high. The college's academic standards rose at the same time.

The first great event of the current post-war years was the taking in, as college accommodation, of the Bull Inn whose handsome Regency frontage dates from its rebuilding in 1828. By 1950 those living at St Catharine's were some four hundred and sixty in all, so that the rooms thus provided were a vast boon to so cramped a college. Undergraduate numbers have now been cut to about three hundred and sixty, with the great increase in post-graduates which is common to all Cambridge colleges.

The sciences and engineering are popular subjects in the college, so too are English literature and Modern languages. A study of particular note in

St Catharine's is, and has long been, geography; one finds, in Universities up and down this country and the rest of the world, that several geography professors and lecturers are St Catharine's men. Athletics are still important, though somewhat less so than before 1939; there has been a certain swing from the Rugby field to the river.

The great feature of life in present-day St Catharine's is the development scheme which has been undertaken jointly with King's. The very fact of such collaboration between any two Colleges is a new element in Cambridge history. One gathers that this joint action came about very largely because of personal friendships between those in each College who were particularly concerned. One thus sees how much in tune the scheme is with the spirit and actuality of College history in Cambridge.

The new work, completed in 1967 behind the early nineteenth-century façade of the Bull Hotel (which still survives), unfortunately involved the demolition of the oldest block in the College, the Gostlin Building of 1634; this was, however, found to be in a very bad state of internal repair. St Catharine's has, however, gained much from its share in the new venture, and is well satisfied with the results. Though some St Catharine's men still have to live out of College, many new sets have been provided, along with a graduates' parlour, a new sick bay, and space for conferences. The most important change has been the building of a new and spacious hall, with new kitchens and some sets of rooms over the site of the Gostlin Building. The new hall, with a shallow oriel at one end and a gallery at one side, seems somewhat dark by daylight but is impressively capacious. The old hall has been horizontally split into a Senior Combination Room and an upstairs library. Another part of the scheme is the feature, new in any Cambridge College, of a large subterranean car park, largely for the College servants. St Catharine's is thus the first Cambridge College, bar blissfully spacious Jesus, to have such a facility within its own grounds.

During this year of 1973 St Catharine's will commemorate the 500th anniversary of its foundation by Robert Wodelarke. Plans have been made for balls, dinners, and a quincentenary concert by the College Musical Society, while Yehudi Menuhin, who is one of the College's Honorary Fellows, will bring an orchestra to give a special concert in the Senate House. A medal and some hand-engraved crystal goblets are to be produced, as also is an important volume of quincentenary essays on the College and its patron saint.

JESUS

FROM the founding of St Catharine's to the commencement of Downing not one Cambridge college came into being on a site not previously occupied by some academic institution, convent, or hospital. Some of the seven colleges founded between 1473 and 1596 retain unsubstantial traces of their predecessors. Elsewhere, as at Magdalene and Trinity, buildings put up for previous foundations are an important part of the present scene. But nowhere has the former state of affairs been more crucial for the appearance, and even for the character, of the later college than at Jesus.

The Dominicans and the Franciscans are somewhat thin memories at Emmanuel and Sidney, while the remains of God's House are heavily overladen at Christ's. But St Radegund's Priory of Benedictine nuns matters much to the College of the Blessed Mary the Virgin, St John the Evangelist, and the glorious virgin St Radegund, 'commonly known', from an early date, as Jesus College.

St Radegund's Priory was founded, on a small scale and by unknown persons, about 1130. Its original site was part of the present college, but in a few more years, perhaps about 1159, the nuns got a royal benefaction which much enlarged their territory and which has been of immense importance for the character and well being of Jesus College. For King Malcolm IV of Scotland, who was also Earl of Huntingdon and who had interests in England's eastern counties, gave the nuns ten acres adjoining their existing land; a church was to be built on a part of the newly presented ground. By a curious coincidence King Malcolm also helped the Oxford priory of St Frideswide, whose church, now serving both as Oxford's cathedral and as the Chapel of Christ Church, is the other 'Oxbridge' college chapel of obviously Norman origins.

The nuns of St Radegund now had a site amply large enough for the usual monastic complex of a church and its adjacent claustral buildings. Some of the Norman work remains, but the best survivals of the priory are 'Early English' Gothic of the thirteenth century.

Though the lands of St Radegund's in and near Cambridge are now, with modern changes in their economic value, of the utmost importance to Jesus College the medieval nunnery was never rich, or of much note as a religious community. Bar the addition, about 1450, of the top stage of the tower which rose above its noble church little seems to have been done to extend or alter its buildings. By the end of the fifteenth century the property was much decayed; worse still, the nunnery was badly disciplined and its inmates were down to no more than two.

St Radegund's, like many others among England's all too numerous small convents of men or women, was ripe for drastic reform or even for abolition. Some other small priories had already been dissolved, their revenues being used for other religious purposes. Dissolution, and the worthy re-use both of its lands or its buildings, was what happened to St Radegund's. The man mainly responsible was a bishop whose reforming temper was akin to that of some other churchmen who now became prominent in Oxford and Cambridge.

John Alcock became Bishop of Ely in 1486. Earlier on, in 1480–82, he had, as Bishop of Worcester, seen to the disciplinary reorganisation and partial rebuilding of the small priory of Benedictine monks at Little Malvern. Now in 1496–97 he set in train the dissolution of St Radegund's and the foundation, in its buildings and with an income from its endowments, of a small academic college. Alcock's work set a precedent for other and similar operations, most notably when Wolsey planned his great foundation of Cardinal College at Oxford. What Alcock (urged on by William Chubbes of Pembroke who became the first Master of Jesus) did at Cambridge was to divert the revenues of St Radegund's to support a college of a Master, six Fellows, and six boy scholars.

The nunnery buildings were more than ample for such a society. They were repaired, partly cased with brick, and in some cases gutted, refitted, and cleverly adapted for their new purpose. The cruciform nunnery church was cut down so that most of its eastern portion became a splendid chapel. The entire site of St Radegund's was made over to the College, giving Jesus a territory, on the north-eastern outskirts of the town, more ample than that owned by any other Cambridge college. Not only did this site prove spacious enough for all future developments but, as it was outside the town and was set back from the main road which led out towards

Newmarket, it gave Jesus College the peace and tranquillity for which the colleges on the Backs now much envy it. King James I, who visited Jesus in 1615, judged shrewdly when he said that, whereas he would worship in King's and dine in Trinity, he would choose Jesus as his place in Cambridge for sleep and study.

Bishop Alcock died in 1500, too soon for him to guide his new college far on its way. James Stanley, who became Bishop of Ely in 1506, carried on Alcock's work and gave Jesus its new statutes. Other benefactions came in during the first years of the sixteenth century, and an unusual feature of Jesus College was the existence, side by side with the usual academic activities, of a grammar school whose pupils had a preference when the college's Fellows came to be chosen. But the college was small, and far from wealthy, by the time of the great religious changes caused by the Reformation. By this time, however, it had produced a most distinguished *alumnus* in the person of Thomas Cranmer, admitted to Jesus in 1503, a Fellow both before his marriage and only a year after his wife's death, and fully engaged in an academic career before his rise to royal favour and the archbishopric of Canterbury.

Though the religious and liturgical changes of Edward VI's time had their effect in Jesus it seems likely that more of the old ritual was kept up in the chapel than in most other Cambridge Colleges; not for the first time the geographical remoteness of Jesus College from the main centre of University may have had some part in keeping it aloof from more fashionable trends. It was certainly true, in later years, that the college avoided the more extreme changes of the Puritan period. By the time of Elizabeth I more endowments and gifts had come in and the modest numbers of the college's foundationers were soon augmented by an influx of pensioners. One can also see, as in much more recent times, how Jesus College added to its revenues by the shrewd administration of house and land property which had come to it from the possessions of St Radegund's.

The years from Elizabeth I's accession to the outbreak of the Civil War were a time of solid prosperity and increasing reputation. The Anglican settlement was easily accepted in Cranmer's college, but there was little room in Jesus for the innovating Puratinism which coloured most other Colleges in Cambridge's 'eastern belt'. Orthodox Anglicanism remained dominant, and the way was clear for the strikingly Royalist posture of the college in the Civil War. The Master, by then, was Richard Sterne, an able administrator and a devoted Laudian High Churchman whose career, after the sufferings and disturbance caused by the Civil War and the Common-wealth period, ended in the Archbishopric of York. When in 1642 Sterne

QUEENS'. In the original Court, looking North-east

ST CATHARINE'S. The Main Court, as seen from Corpus Christi

JESUS. The Chapel Crossing, from the Master's Garden

CHRIST'S. A View of the Fellow's Building, c. 1640–42

ST JOHN'S. The Main Gate, c. 1511–14

loyally sent most of the college's plate to the king he was soon arrested and was duly deprived of his mastership. No less than fourteen Fellows were ejected, and only two remained to be the colleagues of those who were newly installed. Most Jesus men who fought in the war did so on the royalist side. But undergraduate entries soon started again after the king's defeat, and Jesus was reasonably full when, in 1660, Sterne came back as Master for a short time.

The coming years saw the endowment of many more scholarships in the college, most notably those set up by the widely generous Court official Tobias Rustat, the son of a Jesus man but never himself at a university, whose rich cartouche monument, in the full Baroque taste, adorns the west wall of the ante-chapel at Jesus.

The eighteenth century was mostly an even more stagnant period for Jesus College than it was for the University as a whole. The first half of it was taken up by another of Cambridge's excessively long masterships. Dr Charles Ashton, a scholarly but intensely retiring man, held his post from 1701 to 1752; among the more notable incidents in his long reign was the admission, in 1733, of Lawrence Sterne, the great grandson of the Archbishop and the future author of *Tristram Shandy*.

The numbers of those coming up to Jesus fell terribly in this century, and of those who did come up only about half proceeded to degrees. There was thus no need to enlarge the college's buildings. Nor did Jesus, like Peterhouse, Trinity Hall, and some other colleges, reface any of its medieval blocks with Palladian stonework, though many of Alcock's mullioned windows were replaced by the rectangular, sashed openings normal in English Georgian building work.

Patristic theology was the field of study wherein the senior members of Jesus won the most distinction, mathematics and physics being of little account in a college whose isolation in the University became something more than geographical. Yet Jesus College saw a great intellectual revival towards the end of the eighteenth century. Personalities, like that of Dr Richard Beadon, who became Master in 1781, were the key to the change, while much of the new liveliness which reached the college of the strictly Anglican parson-economist T. R. Malthus came from men whose beliefs were eventually Unitarian. The disputes which surrounded these disbelievers in the Trinity in a way anticipated the controversies which enlivened the Cambridge of Darwin and Leslie Stephen. William Frend, the convert to Unitarianism whose religious and political opinions caused his expulsion from the college in 1793, was important not only for himself but because he converted Samuel Taylor Coleridge, who was then a Jesus undergraduate, to his Unitarian belief.

The atmosphere of controversy, and of lively discussion, which was then marked in Jesus made the college an excellent setting, as the poet himself proved, for Coleridge's sparkling conversational talent. Coleridge, after a chequered Cambridge career, finally left Jesus in 1794.

Jesus College shared, even more than most others in Cambridge, in the entry boom which soon followed the end of the Napoleonic War. It was, in the circumstances, surprising that it only extended its buildings by one large staircase. Decline again set in under Dr French who became Master in 1820, though some important changes came in his last few years of office. New statutes of 1841 meant that only six Jesus Fellows need now be in Orders. Soon after that year the restoration of the chapel was taken in hand, and a gradual, artistically unusual process was started whereby Jesus chapel is a building whose nineteenth-century alterations are of as much aesthetic importance as its medieval work. The restoration was started in 1845, the leading spirits being two Fellows who had come under Tractarian and Camden Society influences. Augustus Pugin, the arch-ecclesiologist, was in time asked to supervise the work, while these changes in a High Church direction had their musical side when Gregorian intoning was heard in the chapel services.

By 1850 the Master of Jesus was Dr George Corrie, whose death in office, in 1885 and aged 92, made him the oldest holder of this particular college headship. A convinced Evangelical and a conservative for whom, to quote D. A. Winstanley, 'the last ditch was his spiritual home', he was well known for his dogged opposition to such things as college or University reform and Sunday excursion trains on the railways. Yet many changes came both to the University and to Jesus College in Dr Corrie's time, among them the freedom of all Fellows to marry.

Those resident in Jesus now increased in a spectacular way and when, about 1880, the College had 200 undergraduates it was the third largest in Cambridge. New buildings, very easy to site in so spacious a college, were put up and started to create the present layout of the more modern courts. This was also the period when rowing got established as the sport which is the special glory and distinction of Jesus. The achievements of Jesus men on the river are most appropriate for a college whose location makes it the only one in Cambridge whose boathouse can be seen from one of its own courts.

Between the 1800s and the outbreak of the second World War one comes to the modern story of Jesus College. Many Jesus men were the sons of clergy and a large, though gradually declining proportion of them went on to take Anglican Orders. Mathematics was long the leading subject for those who read for honours, and the great rise of historical studies in Jesus started well in the present century.

The college was apt to be split between some of those who rowed and the majority of the college who did not. Among the rowing men the outstanding figure, particularly as a coach, was the Australian Steve Fairbairn, and many Australians came to Jesus to row under his tuition. In addition, several Jesus men obtained high academic honours, while the names of J. Bronowski, V. C. Clinton Baddeley, Alistair Cooke, and Peter Masefield suggest a wide variety of interests and pursuits. Bernard Manning—historian, tutor, and prominent Congregationalist—was among the best known and best loved Cambridge figures of his time. Arthur Gray, who was Master from 1912 to 1940, had few rivals in his knowledge both of the town and of the University of Cambridge.

Since 1945 a subtle but definite change has come over the life of Jesus College. All over the University admission is now more hardly come by, and academic standards are higher than they were. Many of those who used to come up mainly for sporting and social reasons could nowadays no longer be seen in Cambridge; this has meant that Jesus is now no more 'hearty' a college than any other. Its boats still do well on the river, but it is, with about 350 undergraduates, a far better integrated society than it was before the war. Its cultural life, particularly in drama and in the music rendered in the chapel, is far more lively than it was. As in many other colleges science and engineering are very popular subjects, while economics have now gained a recognised position. But it is history, most fittingly in a college with its roots so deep in the past, which is notably strong.

Many improvements have been made to the existing buildings in Jesus, and much has been done to develop, and make more fruitful, the great belt of urban property which largely lies near the actual college; the new buildings of Malcolm Place, along the northern side of King Street, well illustrate this tendency. Lastly, with Mr David Roberts as architect, one has the successful new buildings, at last forsaking Alcock Gothic, of North Court. Finance was what caused the long delay in their provision, for unlike such tightly constrained central colleges as Clare and Caius, Jesus had no problems over an available site. The twelfth-century founders of the priory, and the later gift from a young Scottish king, ensured that Jesus College can easily, when it so desires, house all its members within the boundaries of its founder's time.

CHRIST'S

SOON after 1500 another of Cambridge's great benefactresses set one more college on its way. Yet Christ's was not a wholly new foundation. Much of its area, and some of its endowments, were those of a small college whose arrival at its site near Barnwell Gate was caused by academic activities, and a sweeping royal benefaction, elsewhere in Cambridge. The re-siting of God's House, the construction of its buildings, and the life of study lived there for nearly sixty years, made an important prelude to the generosity of Lady Margaret Beaufort and the wise guidance of Bishop John Fisher.

The origins of Christ's College go back to 1439. For in that year William Bingham, the holder of the London living of St John Zachary, got royal permission to build a house in Cambridge for the reception of grammar students. He did this because he was concerned at the great shortage, in England's provincial schools, of qualified grammar teachers. He fittingly located his establishment in the Cambridge parish whose church had the same dedication as his own in London. God's House, like the Church of St John Zachary, stood on ground now covered by the western part of the chapel at King's.

Bingham's first idea was to hand his grammarians' hostel to the nearby college of Clare Hall. Soon, however, he set it up as a college on its own. A 'Proctor' was to be its head, and its scholars were to reach the respectable number of twenty-four. But very soon, in 1446, the site of God's House was needed by Henry VI for his enlarged plans for King's. Bingham was allowed to buy a spacious site, on open ground close outside Barnwell Gate, for the relocation of his college, and its endowment, like that of King's, was largely made up of the revenues of 'alien' priories taken over by the Crown during the long war with France. Bingham was, moreover, additionally compensated by being given permission to have his scholars instructed, not only in grammar but in other faculties. From 1448, when Henry VI gave God's House its Charter and was styled its joint founder, the little college continued as a normal, and not as a one-subject foundation. Bingham himself remained Proctor till 1451.

Five others followed him. The last, John Syclyng, was of some note in the University as a whole and was a friend of Lady Margaret. The college's activities included 'refresher' lectures to schoolmasters who came up during the long vacation to improve their knowledge. It had a chapel and other collegiate buildings, and though it was a small college it was not the smallest in Cambridge. Yet by about 1500 the time was ripe for the transformation and expansion of God's House.

John Fisher, already most prominent in Cambridge and the Lady Margaret's confessor, became the University's Chancellor in 1504. He now had the chance to push forward the reforms and improvements he must long have had in mind. The first of these, in 1505, turned out to be the refoundation of God's House, with the re-use and augmentation of its buildings and revenues, as Christ's College. Fisher seems to have been the man who diverted the intentions of Henry VII's mother towards the founding of the first of Cambridge's Beaufort Colleges, and to the first of her two acts of realignment whereby a small or struggling institution blossomed out as a major addition to the University's academic strength.

What Fisher and Lady Margaret did was to reconstitute God's House under the name of Christ's College. A Master, twelve Fellows, and forty-seven pupil-scholars made up what was at once a large college, the largest then existing in Cambridge. Half of the Fellows, and nearly half of the poor scholars, were to come from the North of England. As was fitting in a college sponsored by one keen to advance Renaissance learning, provision was made for the study of classical authors, and the grammar tuition which had been the mainstay of God's House was continued in Christ's. Though Fisher's hand predominated in the new college's academic arrangements one may sense a more feminine touch in the provision that the scholars should sleep two, not the usual four, to a room, and that a nurse should be available in times of their sickness.

Though Christ's, like Jesus and St John's was founded before the onset of the Reformation, not much of its history was that of a pre-Reformation college. Its buildings, including some re-used from God's House, were finished soon after Lady Margaret died in 1509. By then the site had been much increased by the lease, from Jesus, of ground once owned by St Radegund's nunnery.

With Fisher long available to guide its fortunes Christ's started prosperously enough. But with the religious changes under Henry VIII, and with Fisher's fall, the college entered a more difficult spell. Its authorities had some trouble, and had to pay many visits to Thomas Cromwell, to maintain their rights to their endowments. Then, after the usual veerings of allegiance under Edward VI, and Mary I, Christ's settled down, under Elizabeth I, as a college whose tone was distinctly Puritan; this was despite the entry of several Catholics who 'conformed' while in residence. Christ's actually became known for Puritanism of a non-conformist, or 'separatist' stamp. When in 1582 it sought the advice of its *alumnus*, Sir Walter Mildmay, over the choice of a Master, and when he became dissatisfied with the election of Edmund Barwell, Mildmay set in train the actions which soon led to his own founding of Emmanuel.

Christ's was prosperous, and had good numbers, in Elizabeth I's reign, with 136 members in 1564 and the high figure of 157 in another nine years. Its prosperity, allied to a less fierce Puritanism and to moderate Royalism, in most of its members, by the crucial year of 1642, continued in the first half of the seventeenth century which was, for most Cambridge colleges, a peak period of power and influence.

John Milton, the most famous Christ's man of his time, entered in 1625, and his close friend Edward King, whom he immortalised in 'Lycidas', was a Fellow in 1630. By 1641 the College's numbers were up to 163; at this time the serene beauty of the Fellows' Building, with mere vestiges of Gothic amid its generally Renaissance style, gave Cambridge a full taste of what John Evelyn called 'exact architecture'.

The Civil War found Christ's less openly Royalist than many other Cambridge Colleges. Its sympathies were balanced, with an equable, openminded, unfanatical temper which seems often to have been typical of its life and outlook. Some of its Fellows lost their posts in the great academic upheaval of 1644. It was, however, typical of Christ's that its Master, from 1654 in the Commonwealth period, throughout Charles II's reign, and down through that of James II until 1688, was Ralph Cudworth. A leading figure among the Cambridge Platonists, he stood for a balanced, philosophical attitude to the raging controversies of his time. He was a devoted, meticulous Master, much concerned over the college's welfare and unready to seek prominence elsewhere. John Covel, his successor, was famed as a great collector of coins and medals. It was in the middle of his Mastership that the chapel was refurnished and transformed, with the soberly Baroque stalls and altarpiece which give it a most dignified interior.

The first half of the eighteenth century saw in Christ's the decay and stagnation which were all too common in Georgian Cambridge. Things improved towards the end of the century. But a small rise in the college's numbers brought little increase in its standards, and the well-known reminiscences of Henry Gunning, who went up to Christ's in 1784, give no impression of an academically vigorous college. Beilby Porteus, the liberal-minded Bishop of London in George III's time, was a Christ's man; so, too, was William Paley, of 'Evidences' fame. Another aspect of the college's eighteenth century history was its connection with the Nelson family, two of the Admiral's brothers and his nephew being Christ's men. Then, in 1793, there came the death, as a pensioner of Christ's, of Captain Cook's son who had only come up that year.

John Kaye, who was Master of Christ's as well as being Bishop of Bristol and then of Lincoln, did much towards the early nineteenth-century reform of his college. Numbers went up in his time, particularly with the rush of Cambridge entrants soon after the Napoleonic War. Late in Kaye's mastership in 1827, Charles Darwin came up to Christ's; he admitted that his studies there brought him little profit. Reform continued throughout the nineteenth century. Many improvements were made in the college's finances and business management, while new statutes of 1860 allowed five of the Fellows to be laymen. Scientific studies were encouraged, but progress was checked, as it was elsewhere in Cambridge, by the effect on the income of Christ's of the long agricultural depression which started in 1879. Students from India and other Commonwealth countries, among them Jan Christian Smuts, came to Christ's in the early years of this century, and the college's liberal traditions helped it to welcome as its members most of the Roman Catholic priests, whether Downside Benedictines or secular clergy at St Edmund's House, who came to Cambridge to read for degrees.

The size and wealth of Christ's increased after 1918. In the years between the wars, with over 350 undergraduate members in 1926, it ranked among Cambridge's larger colleges. A still higher peak of 452 came in 1952, at the time when Cambridge was flooded with its post-war rush of entrants. Undergraduate numbers at Christ's are now down to about 400, with the College's Fellows more than doubled since the 1930s and nearly eighty post-graduates on various forms of research. As in some other Cambridge colleges, those reading science and engineering at Christ's make up about half its numbers. This was so before the war, and although classics and theology are weaker, and English Literature is stronger than in the 1930s, no drastic change has come over the relative numbers of Christ's men reading each subject.

The first post-war additions to the college buildings came with two blocks, in a predictably neo-Georgian idiom, by the late Sir Albert

Richardson. A far more contemporary style was used by Mr Denys Lasdun for the new building, reaching back as far as King Street and containing some 250 sets as well as various parlours; with its recent completion Christ's has achieved the ambition, now common among Cambridge Colleges, of having almost all its members living in. The inner side, with its receding tiers and terraces giving some reminiscence of pre-Columbian pyramid architecture, is striking, and not unpleasing with its well-finished concrete and nicely detailed gutters. But the back of the new block, with an irregularly composed street frontage of shops and parking space, towers in an aggressive dominance over King Street which was once known as Wall's Lane; the effect, on both sides of a highway once charming in its small-town intimacy, is made worse by the recession of building lines imposed by the planning authorities.

My final point on Christ's is of a literary nature. Lord Snow is a Christ's man, and his novels have given thousands of his readers their image of 'Oxbridge' college life. He never gives a fictional name to the Cambridge college of his novels, but anyone who knows Cambridge at once recognises Christ's as the setting for his pages. One feels, however, that their author would have done better had he set his characters in a feigned college with appropriately invented name, and not in the college 'down Petty Cury' whose site can be none other than that chosen by William Bingham when in the fifteenth century he had to re-site God's House.

ST JOHN'S

THE earliest planning of Cambridge's second Beaufort college takes us almost as far back as the foundation of Christ's. Both Christ's and the great college of St John the Evangelist have to be seen as early fruits of Bishop Fisher's policy for the reinvigoration, under his forward-looking Chancellorship which started in 1504, of the whole University.

If one reckons, as I tend to do myself, that the real history of any corporate institution starts with the first informal, yet seriously intended discussions on the part of its originators, the earliest days of St John's may have been in 1505, the year when Fisher and Lady Margaret Beaufort gave God's House a new lease of life as Christ's College. At St John's the pattern of reorganisation was closer to that of Bishop Alcock at Jesus. For while Christ's involved the continuance of a small, yet reasonably effective college the setting up of St John's meant the extinction of a decayed religious house, with the use of its endowments and buildings to launch a pious institution of a different kind.

The establishment on which Bishop Fisher cast his reforming eye was the old hospital of St John the Evangelist. This had been founded, as an almshouse and as a place for the care of the sick, about 1200. The brethren who ran it lived, as did those of some other hospitals in medieval England, according to the flexible 'Rule of St Augustine'. Late in the thirteenth century it had seen the important academic venture whereby Bishop Balsham of Ely had placed his non-monastic scholars in the hospital buildings. This 'doubling up' caused dissension between the brethren and the academics. The scheme failed, and in four more years the bishop moved his scholars to the two houses which stood on part of the site of Peterhouse. The one relic of Balsham's proposed arrangement was the splendid collegiate chapel, in the 'geometrical' Gothic which prevailed about 1280, which the bishop seems to have built for the joint use of the almsmen and the scholars.

St John's Hospital was left, for more than two hundred years, to continue its charitable work. That work, so it seems, was in the reign of Henry VII being done in a penurious and unsatisfactory way. Fisher had no more hesitation than Alcock had displayed over St Radegund's nunnery in diverting the hospital's modest assets to other purposes more suitable for an age when new currents of thought and learning were reaching England from the Continental sources of the Renaissance. But his own resources, and those of the University itself, fell short of his needs. He turned again to the great lady who had, at his instigation, become the titular foundress of Christ's.

The year 1505 was probably that in which Fisher, Lady Margaret and their advisers discussed the conversion of St John's Hospital into an academic college. In the next four years Lady Margaret spoke much of the project, and in March of 1509 she made a preliminary agreement with her relative, Bishop Stanley of Ely. Yet much remained to be done when at the end of June in that same year Lady Margaret died. In particular, the wording of her will made no provision for the founding of any such college. Its effective commencement depended on the pertinacious energy of Bishop Fisher, who was Lady Margaret's executor, and on a commonsense interpretation of what were her known intentions.

By 1511 Fisher had got the consent of the Pope, of Bishop Stanley, and of the new King Henry VIII, for the suppression of the hospital, for the departure of its brethren, and for the formal foundation of the new college. Building work started at once. The splendid chapel of the hospital, which may well have been in poor condition, was kept for the college. It had to be repaired and adapted very much as the choir of St Radegund's was made suitable for its new use as the chapel of Jesus, so that its general appearance became that of a simple late Perpendicular building.

Some other old hospital buildings were also reused, but in the main the college's first court was splendidly new built, in clunch faced with diapered red brick, as Cambridge's finest and most complete piece of late medieval collegiate planning. In its design, and in its lavish Beaufort references, the gate tower bore obvious resemblance to that of the other Fisher-Beaufort college. Another pleasing feature which St John's shared with Christ's was the richly adorned first-floor oriel window from which the Master, in his lodge, could keep an eye on the whole court. The oriel at St John's, unlike the one at Christ's in that it has kept its early Tudor mullions, was happily reinstated, to overlook the Master's riverside garden, when the mid-Victorian lodge was built along with the new chapel.

The first court of St John's was finished about 1520, and in a few more years the college's increasing numbers obliged it to put up a small second court. For financial reasons, which I shall soon explain, its Fellows were fewer in number than the large figure of fifty intended by Lady Margaret. But it was soon the largest college in Cambridge and by 1545 its membership rose to 152.

It was a great blessing that Fisher lived on for more than twenty years after the opening date of 1511 to guide the fortunes of St John's. In 1535, at the time of his political fall, and even as he awaited death on the scaffold, the college touchingly remembered its gratitude to the man to whom it owed its very livelihood and the foundations of its vigorous life of scholarship. Fisher had, indeed, been a great helper and counsellor in the college's unexpectedly difficult early years. As the foundress had failed to mention St John's in her will, doubts soon arose over the period during which the college, rather than the King, might receive the income from some of her estates. St John's had to yield up the lands, and some money promised from other sources by Henry VIII fell short of the expected sum. In the end, however, Fisher was able to spend sums from Lady Margaret's other property. He obtained new benefactions and, in an anticipation of Wolsey's financing of Christ Church at Oxford, obtained the dissolution of two small nunneries and of another hospital so that St John's might enjoy their revenues.

By 1535 the college's income of more than £500 a year was easily the second largest of any Cambridge college. Its reputation for scholarship stood high, particularly under Nicholas Metcalfe, who became Master in 1518, and Greek studies were specially strong. Religious education remained the college's fundamental purpose, and the North of England, sending such important recruits as Roger Ascham who became tutor to the future Queen Elizabeth I, was a more prominent recruiting ground for Johnians than the South. Roger Ascham was among those at St John's who fully accepted the teachings of the Reformation, and the years after 1537, when Metcalfe retired, were as full of controversy and unsettlement as in many other Cambridge colleges.

The men from the northern counties seem on the whole to have supported the older doctrines, which were anyhow strong in that part of England, so much so that new Statutes given in 1545 restricted their number to not more than half of those holding Fellowships in the college.

From then onwards Reformed opinions gained ground at St John's, with outright Puritanism strong in Elizabeth I's time. The Geneva Psalter was for a few years used in the chapel, though the Prayer Book liturgy soon regained its place. 'Official' or 'Settlement' Protestantism became dominant in the college—appropriately enough when Lord Treasurer Burghley was the most eminent Johnian, and when the college had attracted many of the men whose new ideas and fresh lines of thought did much to mould the character of the Elizabethan age. Burghley took a hand in the running of St John's, arranging for the giving of new statutes in 1580 and on three occasions using his great influence in the nomination of a Master.

By the end of the century the Puritan tide, which had risen high at St John's, was well on the wane, and the last years of Elizabeth I's reign saw St John's busy, with decisive financial help from Mary, Countess of Shrewsbury, on the building of the large, regularly designed second court which was its answer to Great Court in the neighbouring and rival college of Trinity. Its numbers by now stood at about 300, and they continued to increase in the coming century.

The seventeenth century saw continuing prosperity at St John's. Still the largest college in Cambridge, it found that its numerous members who were the sons of noblemen and landed gentry were well balanced by the large number of more humbly born men whose fathers were artisans, farmers, or poor clergy; the time for Cambridge's social exclusiveness still lay well ahead. Increasing 'Laudianism' marked the religious practice of the chapel, where Laudian decorations and furnishings (in a few more years demolished by William Dowsing) were notably prominent.

Strong Royalism accompanied so 'high' a level of churchmanship and, when in 1644 the time came for Parliamentarian purges and ejections, twenty-nine of the Fellows of St John's lost their posts as well as Dr Beale the Master. Such severity inevitably produced its own sharp reaction. After 1660, with the Stuart dynasty restored to power, and with the Church of England again ascendant, St John's settled down to its long spell of intense Toryism in its politics and of High Anglicanism in its religious inclinations.

For so Royalist a college as St John's the Restoration age was naturally a boom time of long-delayed reward. The college's membership, in 1672, stood at the high figure of 373. Such prosperity now called for the attractive completion, all ready in a few more years for its inclusion in Loggan's perspective view, of the third court whose northern side was already made up of the fine Jacobean Gothic library range.

The period was one of staunch Toryism and of its accompanying High Anglicanism, and it was no surprise when in William III's time the defiant

Non-Jurors of St John's equalled those produced by all the other Colleges of Cambridge. By a ruling of 1693 no less than twenty Fellows of St John's were down for ejection. But in a manner very typical of Cambridge's easy-going toleration they (or rather the six of them still on the list in another twenty-four years) were not actually removed till 1717.

Among the six stalwarts who tenaciously remained in college was the eminent and scholarly Thomas Baker, the historian of St John's who described himself as *socius ejectus* but who lived on in his rooms, despite the loss of his Fellowship, for another twenty-three years. He died in 1740, leaving his fine library, and a memory of gratitude, to the college he loved. Another Johnian of the late seventeenth century became better known after his migration to Trinity. One must however, remember that the Yorkshire-man Richard Bentley was entered at St John's when he first came up in 1676. He did outstandingly well in his studies and, had it not been for the firm occupation, by others from his own county, of the college's two Fellowships which were earmarked for Yorkshiremen, he might have lived out his academic life in the Senior Combination Room of St John's and not, to the rival College's discomfiture, in the Lodge at Trinity.

For much of the Georgian period St John's remained the largest College in Cambridge. But by 1800 its undergraduate numbers were down to about 120, and the college had shared deeply in Cambridge's eighteenth-century decline. The diehard Toryism of the Jacobite years was somewhat blunted by the time that the Duke of Newcastle, with his vast and shrewdly managed Whig patronage, was dominant in the University. St John's also narrowed its social field of entry, moving closer to the stage of affairs in which the sons of poor or lower middle-class parents found it ever harder to get to Cambridge. The Johnians of the eighteenth century included several from Colonial North America, and some who were the sons of planters in the West Indies.

By the last years of the eighteenth century St John's had seen some beginnings of reform. College examinations were started so as to check on the undergraduate's progress, religious observances tightened up, and more attention was given to the quality of college teaching. After a few vigorous years there was a slackening in the college's progress; Wordsworth's 'Prelude', in its passages describing his life as a Johnian after his coming up in 1787, does not give one the impression of a very hard-working college. The future poet had rooms, in the western range of the first court, which lay above the college kitchens, being hot and noisy from the heat and clatter of cooking operations, with added disturbance from the almost adjacent chapel bell of Trinity. No new buildings were needed by a much diminished college, but a start was made, under Capability Brown, on the formal layout of the Wilderness across the river.

Clarkson, the anti-slavery propagandist, and Wilberforce, who secured the slave trade's abolition by Parliament, were both of them Johnians of the late eighteenth century, while the Evangelical fervour of Charles Simeon found Johnian disciples, near and soon after the turn of the century, in the missionary Henry Martyn, and in Francis Close who was so greatly to mould the religious and social character of the spa town of Cheltenham.

Though the early years of last century saw St John's surpassed in size by Trinity, the college expanded, as did others in Cambridge, soon after the end of the Napoleonic War.

An important reform, dating from 1820, was the change, in the arrangements for the college's foundation Fellowships, whereby they could now be awarded without regard to their holders' native counties. The other big change was by way of new accommodation. In the building of its New Court St John's became the first college on the east side of the Cam to build really substantially across the river. The large early Revival Gothic buildings by Rickman and Hutchinson were finished, for the sum of £78,000, in 1831. They were reached, from the third court, by the covered 'Bridge of Sighs', a Gothic version of a 'Palladian' bridge which is among the most famous, and is certainly the most photographed, nineteenth-century structure in Cambridge.

By the middle of the nineteenth century 371 undergraduates were up at St John's and mathematics remained the chief subject among the minority of Johnians who read for honours.

In the middle decades of last century, when Cambridge was enmeshed in the painfully controversial processes which in time led to college and University reform, St John's was a college where the new movements were in the end more welcome than in most others. At first, in the 1830s when Whewell of Trinity put forward reform proposals, St John's held back during the Masterships of James Wood and Ralph Tatham. But when the Royal Commission of 1850 led to the Cambridge University Act of 1856, and to the gradual revision of University and college statutes, St John's contained a leading reformer in William Henry Bateson, whose mastership ran from 1857 to 1881. From his undergraduate days, and as senior bursar, he had fought for change in the college itself, and his secretaryship of the Royal Commission was a logical prelude to the reforms of his mastership.

An important innovation was the building by St John's of its own chemical laboratory. The college's numbers fell a little towards the end of the century, and there were considerable financial difficulties. But compensations came with a fine athletic tradition, and in a widening of the range of studies pursued by Johnians. Another important event, complete in 1869, was the sad demolition of the old chapel and its replacement, at a time when compulsory chapel was still the rule, and when college numbers were still too large for the old building, by the bulky mid-Victorian Gothic structure designed by Sir George Gilbert Scott. The body of this chapel is a doubtful aesthetic success. But the tower, with its obvious derivation from that of Pershore Abbey, is a real enhancement of the Cambridge skyline, which in the main falls far short of the silhouette of the University city where spires are said to dream. The lengthening of the hall, in an early Tudor Gothic idiom the same as that of its original portion, was far more pleasingly done.

The last years of the nineteenth century, and the years up to the outbreak of the first World War, saw St John's gradually recovering, by careful husbandry and a wise policy of property investment, from the financial troubles which had set in with the great agricultural depression of 1879. Its numerical membership was slower to recuperate and the college had only 274 junior members in 1914.

The subjects read in the college broadened out, as they did in the University as a whole. Scientists increased greatly and historians gained a considerable place in the college, where Coulton and Previté-Orton once resided. Professor Edward Miller, the most recent historian of the college, has pointed out that among those who left St John's, civil servants and professional men were more numerous, and clergymen fewer, than in mid-Victorian times.

The years soon after 1918 saw St John's regaining its numbers, not only from the inevitable contraction of the war itself but from its decline in the period before 1914. In the 1930s it had nearly five hundred junior members, and since then it has remained a large college, long the second largest in Cambridge and still second only to Trinity. The great changes in its teaching, and in the advance of scientific subjects, corresponded to what was happening generally in Cambridge. On its own initiative, and ahead of the time when the University itself encouraged a vast increase in its post-graduate and research students, St John's much expanded this element in its membership. Its Fellows also increased in number. M.P. Charlesworth and T. R. Glover stood out as leading personalities among them, while Ernest Alfred Benians was most successful, both as a tutor and as the first historian to hold the mastership of St John's. New buildings in Chapel Court, designed to provide more rooms for those living in college were finished about a year after the outbreak of the Second World War.

Since 1945 the history of St John's has combined restoration work and new building with its efforts, corresponding to those which other colleges have made, to adapt its tuition and its social life to the new needs of the post-war age. Its Fellows have increased to about ninety; with so large a teaching body, and with the college's undergraduates still numbering over five hundred, Johnians can study in many faculties, with classics strong as well as such heavily frequented subjects as mathematics and engineering.

The total community of St John's, including some one hundred and fifty post-graduates, stands at about 750. As about 550 of these men are living in college St John's can at the moment claim to have the largest resident body of any college in Cambridge. It has still, in the last few years, been able to count many eminent men among its members; the names of Nikolaus Pevsner (as Slade Professor of Fine Art), Glyn Daniel, and Fred Hoyle spring readily to mind. Professor Pevsner had rooms amid the Rickmanesque Revival Gothic of New Court. It is behind that court, near the mouth of the Bin Brook and on the site of the fishponds once used by St John's Hospital, that the college's latest, ambitious building operations have now been finished.

The earlier post-war years were taken up with delicate, loving and costly works of renovation and rebuilding—in particular on the kitchen range and on the Shrewsbury tower, where the crumbling of the inner core of clunch meant total dismantling and subsequent renewal. The newest buildings, by the London architects Powell and Moya, were made possible by large benefactions from the Cripps Trust, one of its members, Mr Humphrey Cripps, being a Johnian. The Cripps Building provides almost two hundred undergraduate sets, and a few for Fellows.

Much has also been done to provide more room for post-graduates, including accommodation for those who are married. As an addition to the ground now covered by the Cripps Building St John's has now bought the land, originally taken up by Bishop Walter de Merton for the possible siting of a Cambridge college and for seven centuries the property of the Oxford college which bears his name. Among the buildings on this site is the Transitional Norman 'Stone House' (later, for some odd reason, known as the School of Pythagoras), which was built by the wealthy Dunning family a few years before St John's Hospital was founded, and a short time before scholars first came to Cambridge. This building much needed repair and has now been restored for its modern use as two community rooms, with space within its ancient walls for small meetings and chamber concerts. Excavation beneath its cellar floor revealed some of the bases of the round columns which once upheld its vault. St John's most recent purchase has thus given the college its oldest building within the long site which now stretches from Trinity to Northampton Streets.

One has, in these latest events in the history of a college, whose site continuity goes back to about 1200, a fascinating cat's cradle of historic ironies. For its purchase of this Oxford outpost in Cambridge takes one back to the time when Bishop Balsham, in his efforts to found a Cambridge college for the training of non-monastic clergy, modelled his statutes on those of Bishop Merton's Oxford foundation. One also recalls that, had he been successful with the first of his chosen locations, a college of St John the Evangelist might well have arisen in Cambridge more than two centuries before Bishop Fisher transformed St John's Hospital into the great and varied college which is now so much a part of the central Cambridge scene.

MAGDALENE

THE early years of Magdalene College were in some continuity with the history of the Benedictine College, known as Buckingham College, whose buildings housed the foundation made in the last years of Henry VIII's reign. In addition, a parallel can soon be found with the origins of two Colleges at Oxford.

Magdalene's founder was surely among the least attractive men who ever set a Cambridge college on its way. Thomas Audley, an Essex man who may have been a lay student at Buckingham College, was among the most thrusting of the careerists who made their way, amid the varying events of Henry VIII's reign, to the top positions. He was a lawyer and politician who closely and ruthlessly served the purposes of a king set on moulding England's ecclesiastical allegiance in such a way as to serve religious purposes and to forward his dynasty's political ends. Audley was Speaker in 1539 and soon became Chancellor of the Court of Augmentations which later handled the gathering in and redistribution of the revenues obtained from the dissolved monasteries. He himself obtained much monastic land, notably from the possessions of Walden Abbey in Essex and of the Augustinian Priory, then just outside London, of Holy Trinity, Aldgate.

From 1533 till his death Audley was Lord Chancellor; as such he behaved with much harshness at the trials both of his predecessor, Sir Thomas More, and of Queen Anne Boleyn. He was twice married. But as he had no male issue he turned his thoughts, when in his fifties and perhaps expecting an early death, to some benefaction which would aid the cause of learning. As the new owner of the Walden Abbey estate, and perhaps as an *alumnus* of Buckingham College, he naturally turned to the empty and incomplete buildings at Cambridge to which student monks of Walden Abbey had once repaired. In 1542, having acquired the three-sided Buckingham court across the river from all the other colleges in Cambridge, he began its refoundation as Magdalen College (the final 'e' came in the nineteenth century). Two years later he died. His estate at Audley End eventually passed, through his daughter and sole heiress who became Duchess of Norfolk, to that branch of the Howard family which obtained the Earldom of Suffolk. The main work of foundation at Magdalene fell to Audley's executors, and especially to Sir Thomas Pope who has a claim to be considered the college's main promoter.

The history of Magdalene's first few years is obscure, and they may well have been troubled. Henry VIII's temporary threat to all academic colleges came in 1546, and Edward VI's short reign was full of trouble and disturbance. Then in 1554, with Mary I seeming firm on the throne, and with Sir Thomas Pope at hand to guide Magdalene's fortunes, the slenderly endowed little college got its first statutes which may well have been the work of Pope himself.

Sir Thomas Pope was an important man for the history of colleges both in Oxford and Cambridge. He had been an official in the Court of Chancery. He there became the personal clerk and close friend of Lord Audley, who named him one of his executors. He was also Treasurer of the Court of Augmentations; as such he was well placed to obtain ex-monastic property and by the mid-1550s he had, in fact, got large amounts of it. But his religious opinions remained staunchly Catholic, and he was among the owners of one-time monastic property who was ready to disgorge some of it for other religious purposes.

Such an act was his foundation—in 1555 and in some of the buildings which had been those of the Benedictine establishment of Durham College —of Trinity College at Oxford. As one of Audley's executors, his work for Magdalene at Cambridge turned out to be of much the same kind. It seems likely that this supporter of Mary I's religious policy was mainly, if not wholly, responsible for the Magdalene Statutes of 1554. Their strong emphasis on theological studies made it clear that the little college was due to play its part in supplying educated Catholic clergy to combat Lutheran and Calvinist teaching. The same purpose was expressed in the nearly-contemporary Oxford foundation of St John the Baptist, while a modern writer on the Oxford Trinity College points out the resemblances between the statutes of Magdalene and those of Sir Thomas Pope's Oxford foundation. The three colleges, all set up in buildings which had once been monastic houses of learning, can be seen as a part of the 'Counter Reformation' church policy of Mary Tudor and Cardinal Pole. The frustration of that policy came sooner than could have been expected, with the deaths, on the same day in 1558, of the Queen and of the Cardinal.

The Elizabethan history of Magdalene was comparatively uneventful; in so far as notable things occurred they were largely of ill omen. The religious character of the college changed, as could have been expected, with the consolidation of Elizabeth's church settlement. Magdalene's resident members numbered forty-nine in 1573. This was in the unhappy mastership of Roger Kelke, a period marked by severe dissensions among the college's senior members and, worse still, by the permanent loss of the property on the edge of the City of London, which had been given by its founder.

Lord Audley's foundation of the college had included the provision, unique among the conditions accompanying the foundation of any Cambridge college, that the Visitorship of Magdalene, and the appointment of its Masters, should rest with the successive owners of his newly gained estate of Audley End. This meant, in practice, that his successors in that splendid Essex property had a large say in the control of the college. More promisingly for Magdalene, its founder gave it some of his land which had once belonged to Holy Trinity Priory near Aldgate. In 1542 the expansion of London had not yet made this property really valuable. In 1575 the garden property in Aldgate was granted, perhaps at Lord Burghley's instigation, to the Queen, being leased at once to a Genoese merchant who lived in London, who had lent Elizabeth a large sum of money, and who promptly emerged as a 'developer' and built many houses on this and other London sites.

Magdalene never recovered the property whose retention could have made it among the richest colleges in Cambridge. For the moment, it had to be content with a financial position very much at the other end of the scale.

By the end of Elizabeth I's reign the fortunes of Magdalene had in part recovered. The efficient mastership of Thomas Nevile (more famed for his headship of Trinity) seems to have inspired enough confidence for new benefactors to come forward. Chief among these was Sir Christopher Wray, a Magdalene man who as Chief Justice of the Queen's Bench sentenced the Jesuit Edmund Campion and was an assessor at the trial of Mary Queen of Scots. Apart from his useful endowments Wray largely paid for the completion of the college's first court with the range, having an Elizabethan Renaissance doorway, which lies along the street.

In the seventeenth century Magdalene shared in the prosperity and rising prestige of all Cambridge colleges. Magdalene men of that period included Henry Dunster who became the first President of Harvard, and the college had 120 members (including a majority of pensioners) in 1621. New accommodation was soon planned, and among other benefactions the second Earl of Suffolk left money towards the new building which is often known, from its most famous contents, as the Pepysian Library. Money was still being raised in 1640 for this charming block, in some details recalling Nevile's Court at Trinity, but its completion was delayed till well after the Civil War.

The Civil War and the Commonwealth brought Magdalene the troubles inevitable for a mainly Royalist, though not pronouncedly 'Laudian' college. Nine Fellows were soon ejected, and Edward Rainbow the Master went in 1650. At the Restoration he was reinstated, and later was one of the numerous Magdalene dons who have either been Bishops or Deans of Peterborough. The best known Magdalene man came up during the Commonwealth period, for Samuel Pepys was entered in 1651; one notes with interest that he had first got a sizarship at Trinity Hall. He much loved his quiet little riverside college, but when he died he copied Archbishop Parker at Corpus and did not give his own college the undivided control of his splendid library. For his bequest was to Trinity or Magdalene but, other things being even, to his own college. It was at the death of his nephew and executor that the books, and their unusual cases, came to Magdalene, and when in 1847 they were moved, for a time, to the new master's lodge, the transfer had to have Trinity's consent.

Though in the 1670s Magdalene's numbers were still well below the figure of fifty years before, the Restoration period was one of placid recovery. John Peachell, who was Master from 1679 to 1690, was known, to Pepys and others, for his addiction to the bottle. Under James II he lost his posts of Vice-Chancellor and Master when the University refused an honorary degree to a Benedictine monk. The Revolution saw his return to Magdalene, but not for long. For when Archbishop Sancroft rebuked him for his drinking habits he went on hunger strike and died as a result.

The eighteenth century was a serene time in Magdalene. Courtly living and good scholarship were combined, and a notably strong mathematical tradition was established. In the 1750s the chapel was redecorated in what Ackermann's print of its interior shows to have been a notably pleasing Georgian Gothic.

Such was its state when Magdalene became a great stronghold of Evangelical churchmanship. Peter Peckard, who became Master in 1781, was a 'rational Christian' who had little personal sympathy with the views now dominant in the college. But he wisely tolerated the trend which William Farish, the Evangelical Senior Tutor, had established, and he would not oppose the Magdalene men whose parents wished 'for a virtuous rather than a fashionable education'. Magdalene filled up with Evangelical ordinands. Many were disciples of Charles Simeon, and like Simeon himself at his parties in King's they nurtured their piety with such copious draughts of tea that Magdalene's first boat on the river became known as 'the tea kettle'. This Evangelical phase eased off as the nineteenth century progressed. An aristocratic flavour re-established itself, but without the loss of high academic standards. At a time when a few Roman Catholics were finding their way to Cambridge (though without taking degrees) the future Cardinal Acton, who was the uncle of Lord Acton, the historian, was at Magdalene for four years from 1819.

By now the Lords Braybrooke owned Audley End, and for ninety-one years from 1813 two successive members of the Neville family held Magdalene's mastership. What could have proved an abuse in fact worked well, and the Rev. Latimer Neville, who was Master from 1853 to 1904, was among the best holders of the post. His brothers, the third, fourth, and fifth Barons all died without male heirs, so that late in life Latimer Neville himself became Lord Braybrooke and was both Master and Visitor of his own college.

Charles Kingsley was at Magdalene in Victorian times. So too, till his rustication after conviction for assault, was Charles Stuart Parnell; he could have returned to college next term but in fact never did so.

The masterships of Stuart Alexander Donaldson and A. C. Benson saw Magdalene maintaining its combined character of a 'social' and a 'reading' college. The present Archbishop of Canterbury, whose father was a Fellow, was there as an undergraduate in the 1920s, while Benson's mastership did much to confirm Magdalene as a college attended by many old Etonians with pronounced social and sporting tastes. These Etonians remained strong in numbers all through the 1930s. Though Magdalene remained small, its accommodation now spread across the street, and the neo-Renaissance range by Lutyens was one block only of what was meant to be a three-sided court opening on to the river.

Soon before the second World War Magdalene's undergraduates had numbered fewer than two hundred. The post-war expansion of the University much increased their number, and in 1956 there were nearly 300. Since then Magdalene's undergraduates (though not post-graduates and research workers) have become fewer, and the college has remained small, with about 270 undergraduates. Its endowed income, as always, has stayed near the bottom of the Cambridge collegiate scale.

Like some other Cambridge colleges Magdalene has become a quieter, harder-working society than it was before 1939. A high proportion of its membership is drawn from public schools. But Eton is not nearly so important a field of recruitment as it was between the wars, and old Marlburians are now nearly as numerous in Magdalene as men from Eton. Classics and medicine are read by fewer Magdalene men than in the 1930s, but natural sciences, economics, and English are all on the increase. Architecture, appropriately in a college which has Mr David Roberts as a Fellow and as the designer of some hostel blocks and its new Master's Lodge, is fairly strong.

For a time, Magdalene built fewer new buildings than some other Cambridge colleges. But much modernisation has occurred in the varied ones of great age, and the clearance of thick ivy has revealed delightful medieval brickwork on the buildings once those of Buckingham College.

Recent expansion has been in the area previously, in part, occupied by Benson Court, and by the converted buildings of Mallory Court whose name comes from the Magdalene man who died, in 1924, in an attempt to scale Mount Everest. The most interestingly modern of these buildings, completed in 1970 in deep red brick, are those of Buckingham Court. Most Magdalene men can now, if they wish, live in College, the great majority of them across the street from the site first chosen by the Benedictines for their student monks and then preserved for academic uses by Lord Audley.

TRINITY

THOSE who know Trinity College, Dublin, are familiar with the idea that a single college of the Oxford and Cambridge type can grow far beyond its original size and yet coincide with a complete University. It was no surprise that Trinity in Dublin was founded, in Elizabethan times, on the model of its Cambridge namesake. For although the Cambridge Trinity has never been the only college in the University, or more than the largest unit in an academic federation, its original size, and its great distinction through long periods of its history, have at times made it seem like a self-contained University within the large site passed on to it by the two older colleges whose work it replaced and enlarged.

In my account of the history of King's Hall, I mentioned the crisis, near the end of Henry VIII's reign, which could have meant the extinction of all the 'Oxbridge' colleges. I explained how Queen Catherine Parr, on a strong appeal from the University authorities, was just in time to persuade her mortally sick husband not to enforce this aspect of the Act for dissolving Colleges, but instead to carry out a long nurtured scheme for the foundation of a great Cambridge College to rival or surpass Christ Church at Oxford.

The result of her entreaties was the suppression of King's Hall and Michaelhouse, the abolition of several academic hostels, and the foundation of Trinity. This was done within the combined site of the two older colleges and by the use of some of their buildings. Trinity College may well regard Queen Catherine Parr as one of its greatest benefactors. It was, perhaps, a misfortune that the King survived the new college's formal inauguration by only a few weeks. Had he lived for a few more years the lay-out, and the early architectural history, of Trinity's first buildings might have been more imposing and less confusing than is actually the case.

MAGDALENE. Renaissance addition; the Pepys Building

TRINITY. The Fountain in Great Court, c. 1600–02; Great Gate behind

The Wars of the Roses had frustrated its founder's plan for King's. Death, and a period of religious change and political confusion had their effect on the early fortunes of Trinity. The combined revenues of King's Hall and Michaelhouse came to a respectable sum, enough to make Trinity one of the richer colleges in Cambridge. But the King decided that this great royal college, with its special continuity with King's Hall which his Plantagenet ancestors had founded, should far surpass any other Cambridge college.

By the grant of some money of his own, and by making over numerous ex-monastic endowments, he vastly increased the real property, and the income, already available to Trinity. By the middle of 1546, some months before the formal Charter of inauguration, his gifts had included the site, and the empty buildings, of Cambridge's Franciscan friary. Its buildings were soon pulled down to provide materials for new building work in Trinity, and its conduit, running in under the river from Madingley Hill, was intercepted within the new college, eventually to give water to the famous fountain in Great Court. Trinity's annual income soon reached the great sum of £1,678. With such resources the college's academic community could be generously planned.

From the beginning Trinity was a notably large college. Provision was first made for a Master (always appointed by the Crown), for fifty graduate Fellows, ten undergraduate scholars, forty grammar scholars (who soon became ordinary undergraduate students) and eight Bible clerks. The college's endowments, and its buildings, were again increased under Mary I; the theological purpose of the original foundation served her purpose as well as it had suited the policy of her father, and the extirpation of 'the perverse opinions of false prophets' was expressed in the wording of her gift. In a few more years, when the college got some new statutes, the numbers in the various classes of its membership were slightly varied. But Trinity remained an endowed society larger than any other one in Cambridge, and the Regius Professors of Hebrew, Greek and Latin were all paid out of its income.

King Henry VIII may possibly, in the last months of his life, have made some grand architectural plan for Trinity which one could have compared with Henry VI's plans for King's or those started by Wolsey for Cardinal College at Oxford. But if any such scheme was evolved it was never attempted, so that the Great Gate of King's Hall and the hall of Michaelhouse survived as better, more stylish buildings than any of those put up in late Tudor Trinity.

Great Court, as finally achieved by Thomas Nevile in his memorable mastership, may in its ground plan have revived some project of the college's earliest days. But in its architectural quality it probably falls well short of what would have been built had the ailing Henry VIII lived to see a comprehensive building plan carried through to completion. In fact, the building of Trinity was a somewhat scrappy process, new work of the 1550s being pulled down to clear the spacious site of Great Court as this was finished by about 1602. The chapel started under Mary I, the impressive hall which was designed by Ralph Symons and which was modelled on that of the Middle Temple, and the canopied fountain in the middle of the enclosure are the court's chief adornments. A more attractive court, blending the survivalist Gothic and the Renaissance styles, was Nevile's Court towards the river. The Master built the eastern part of this court at his own expense. By 1615, when Nevile died, the first building phase at Trinity was over, ample space being provided for a large and fashionable college, about equal in its total numbers to those of its neighbour St John's and so remaining till the Civil War broke out.

In its early days Trinity was almost a colony of St John's, with its first four masters all of them Johnians, and numerous Fellows from St John's as well as those who came through from King's Hall. The same period saw the forging of the college's strong (in the end excessively strong) link with Westminster School. Each year, three Westminster boys had a right to a Trinity scholarship, and by 1700 about a quarter of Trinity's Fellows, irrespective of merit, were Westminster men. A good feature of these early years was the firm establishment, and clear recognition, of the importance of the college tutors; their strong position in Trinity was important for the tutorial system in Cambridge as a whole. Like most Cambridge colleges, Trinity quickly found itself caught up in the religious controversies which soon followed Elizabeth I's 'middle of the road' Church settlement. A large Puritan element vigorously asserted itself in the college. Glass got broken in the chapel, and surplices were discarded as 'abominable rags of superstition'. The Puritan leader, in Trinity as in the whole University, was Thomas Cartwright, a Fellow of the college and the University's Lady Margaret Professor of Divinity. He was sternly opposed by John Whitgift, the Master of Trinity and a future Archbishop of Canterbury, who expelled Cartwright from his fellowship when he refused to take priest's Orders.

Thomas Nevile's mastership was largely concerned with administration and building, and it ended with his death in 1615. The particularly royal character of Trinity had already been stressed, in 1613, when the future King Charles I paid a visit to the college, and still more in the year of Nevile's death when James I and Prince Charles stayed twice in the Master's

Lodge. By now, moreover, the custom had become established whereby the Assize Judges, when on circuit and holding sessions in Cambridge, made it their normal, though unofficial practice to stay in Trinity.

The poet George Herbert came up to Trinity in 1609, and it was natural enough that the college harboured moderate Royalism, not Puritanism of the Emmanuel stamp. Yet combative high churchmanship of the Laudian type was never strong in Trinity; one already saw in the college that balanced, scientific, liberal-minded view of affairs which marked the great College whose sympathies were Whig, and were very distinct from the engrained high Toryism of the great rival college over Trinity's northern wall. But when the Civil War started Trinity's royalism was strong enough for some thirty of its Fellows to suffer ejection. Only four of those put in to fill the vacant places stayed on during the Restoration period which was that of Isaac Newton's residence in Trinity.

Isaac Barrow, a great mathematician and the Master of Trinity from 1672 to 1677, was Newton's teacher and a great influence on his early years. Barrow was a close friend of Sir Christopher Wren, like himself a mathematician, and his chief work, as Master of Trinity, was the starting of the college's splendid pillared library at the riverward end of Nevile's Court. Wren was Barrow's architect, and a circular plan was first proposed but was changed, for financial reasons, to the rectangular plan which is, in fact, more in sympathy with the planning of a college court.

Newton himself, till he left for London in 1696, resided in his famous rooms in Great Court while the new library was going up on the other side of the college. Some of his greatest work, including much of that on the 'Principia', was done while he resided in Trinity, and it was while he was a Fellow that William III suggested his name for the vacant Provostship of King's.

Trinity's membership, by the end of the seventeenth century, was rather less than that of St John's. Despite a large element from the Midlands and the North its fashionable character, with many entrants from London and its close neighbourhood, was still maintained. The privileges accorded to entrants from Westminster School and the 'election' of many Fellows under mandates from the Crown, tended to lessen the college's quality, creating weaknesses all too apparent in the four decades of turmoil which soon followed under the greatest personality among those from outside its own walls who have made Trinity their eventual home.

Richard Bentley's reputation as a scholar and as a divine was deeply established by 1700 when this eminent Johnian became Master of Trinity. His 'Dissertation' on the supposed Epistles of Phalaris, the most famous of all his achievements in the field of classical scholarship, had already appeared. He continued his scholarly activities, but the remaining forty-two years of his life are more worthy of note, for anyone who has to record the story of his adoptive college, for the long, bitter, and tactically successful internal battles which he waged as Master of Trinity. In fairness to Bentley, and as some off-set to the harm which his over-long reign did to the college, one must admit that much was wrong with Trinity as Bentley found it in 1700. The college had much declined since the days when Barrow, and then Newton, had been its most eminent residents. Throughout Bentley's mastership there was no one of the personality, or of the intellectual stature, needed to withstand him.

The Master's first improvements to the Lodge cost far more than anyone, Bentley himself included, foresaw when they were started. One has more-over, to remember, in defence of the changes which Bentley made in his official residence, that in 1700 Trinity awaited as one of its junior members a male heir to the Throne, and that the young Duke of Gloucester (who never resided, but died that year) was to live not in Madingley Hall or in a set in New Court, but as an inmate of the Master's Lodge. That Lodge, as much refurbished by Bentley, was the scene of his happy domestic life with the charming lady whom he married in 1701, of the births of his children and of the death, aged only a few days, of a little son. Bentley's first brushes with the Fellows of Trinity were a small prelude to those which followed. Here again, one has to set them in a wider context. Many of Bentley's policies, particularly those which aimed at widening the range of studies in Trinity, and in making Cambridge a great home of scientific research, were admirable and were far in advance of their time. Had he been of a more co-operative temperament Bentley could have been remembered, in Cambridge, in as good a light as that which shone over Jowett in late Victorian Oxford. But co-operation, particularly with the Fellows of his own college, was not in Bentley's manner. Where he erred so much was in his high-handed contempt of his colleagues, in the way in which such things as his splendid refitting of the chapel choir were done without proper con-sultation or financial control, in the tyrannical way in which he ruled the college from the seclusion of the Lodge, and in his final manipulation of affairs so that for eight years he blithely ignored his actual deprivation from his office.

Bentley could certainly claim, in the last few years of his life, that by good luck in 1714, when the death of Bishop Moore of Ely saved him from certain ejection, by ruthlessness, and by brilliant manoeuvring he had totally secured his position as the unchallenged tyrant of Trinity. What he may not have realised, at a time when all Cambridge was in serious decline, was that the long years of bitter, noisy strife had much hurt Trinity's reputation at a time when no Cambridge college could afford avoidable losses. Though Trinity men, as if in a self-contained University, could now read more subjects their numbers had seriously declined, and the academic standards of the college had actually been cut back by the internal strife which so great a scholar had unhappily caused.

The later years of the eighteenth century were a more placid time for Trinity, and the important changes made to various buildings were achieved with greater harmony than had ever been possible during the Bentley régime. But as the period was one of general academic decline in Cambridge one could not say that Trinity's prosperity much increased. The 1760s, with an average annual entry of no more than twenty-one, saw the lowest point in the college's numbers. But a rise followed, and by about 1790 Trinity had on its books about a third of those resident in the entire University; some of its members, by now, were men from overseas.

After a severe controversy in 1786, its fellowships were awarded as the result of examinations. The intellectual standards among its senior members thus started to rise again, and this was the period when Porson stood out both as a somewhat controversial member of Trinity and as a classical scholar of international renown. Like Bentley, he was of a 'difficult' personality, his main eccentricities being frequent drunkenness and an extreme contempt of his personal appearance.

The late Georgian period saw a great revival in Trinity's fortunes, while in the number of its students the college moved up, above St John's, into the top position in Cambridge which it has since held. Fine classical scholarship long remained a foundation of its eminence, while the college's continued aristocratic and Whig character meant that it readily attracted such entrants as Byron and the future Lord Melbourne.

The roll of famous Trinity men became long and dazzling. Macaulay, Thackeray and Tennyson added new names to Trinity's already large list of literary men, and Tennyson's close friendship with Arthur Henry Hallam led to his writing of 'In Memoriam'. Bulwer Lytton, William Mackworth Praed, and Monckton Milnes were Trinity men whose future activities ranged between literature and politics. As the college's numbers increased new living quarters became a pressing need; in the 1820s the building, between Nevile's Court and Garret Hostel Lane, of Wilkin's Perpendicular Gothic New Court, went far, for some years, to solve the problem.

The Victorian age confirmed the eminence of what was now firmly established as Cambridge's largest college. The range of subjects which its members could study continued to expand, and its senior members included men who could lecture, supervise and research in a wide academic field. Scientific studies became increasingly important in Trinity, and the college built up the position in which it could become the home of Clerk Maxwell, Lord Rayleigh and Lord Rutherford. Jebb and Maitland were of outstanding note in their respective disciplines of classics and constitutional history, and Trinity's enquiring, balanced, liberal-minded tradition appeared in some important religious leaders of Victorian days. Frederick Denison Maurice had been at the college in the 1820s, while the prominent theologians Hort, Lightfoot, and Westcott were all of them Trinity men. During all this time, athletics were becoming more highly organised in Trinity, as elsewhere in Cambridge. The college also continued to be popular in royal and aristocratic circles, and this tradition, along with the friendship of the Prince Consort for William Whewell its Master, made it the obvious college for the Cambridge sojourn of Edward, Prince of Wales.

William Whewell was certainly the leading personality in Victorian Trinity. He is remembered for his prompt re-Gothicising of the eastern side of the Lodge, and for the unattractive though useful courts which he built for the college on a site bought for it across Trinity Street. There was, however, much more to Whewell's mastership than building activity. Domineering in character, temperamentally opposed to change, and a staunch conservative in college affairs, Whewell was none the less one of those who helped on the great nineteenth-century process of University reform. The broadening out of the University curriculum was among his cherished policies, and his backing for the Prince Consort's election as the University's Chancellor was itself an aid to the coming of fresh ideas and new influences. In Trinity itself, the main changes, similar to those carried out in the University as a whole, came after Whewell's death in 1866. Trinity's academic brilliance, and its favoured place as the chief 'social' college in Cambridge, continued after 1866 and for the rest of the last century.

From about 1900, one comes to the story of modern Trinity. Though it was the largest and richest Cambridge college it was strangely slow over the process of physical expansion. Nothing of importance was built in Trinity between 1900 and the beginning of the Second World War, and the college relied heavily on outside lodgings for its many undergraduates. No one doubted the vast academic eminence of a college whose other main element, less studious but none the less characterful, was a main support for such exclusive clubs as the Pitt and the Atheneum.

Lord Acton had lived in Trinity in the late Victorian period, and had foreshadowed his college's brilliant place in the Cambridge history faculty whose reputation was further established, and supremely adorned, by George Macaulay Trevelyan. Sir Stephen Runciman has linked Trinity's name with Byzantine studies while for most of his time as Kennedy Professor of Latin that great Oxford man, A. E. Housman, lived his quiet, neat, secluded life in his rooms in Whewell's Court. Bertrand Russell was also a Trinity resident, while Sir J. J. Thomson and Lord Adrian have been conspicuous among Trinity's many brilliant scientists. These are a few of the more outstanding names; more remarkable, in its way, has been the general level of ability among those who have won Trinity scholarships, or who sat at High Table in the college's great Elizabethan hall.

Many of the changes which have swept over Cambridge since 1945 have had their effect on Trinity. Among them, as also at Oxford, is a general tightening of academic standards, and it is harder now for a man to enter the college merely because his father was there. As in other Cambridge colleges, those reading science in Trinity are more numerous, in proportion to the others, than was once the case, while the increase in the college's scientific Fellows is as much caused by greater specialisation, within the field of science, as by the increase which has certainly occurred in the pupils of those particular dons. As Trinity is a wealthy college, it has been able to increase the number of its Fellows; they now number over 100 as against a pre-war figure of some sixty. The college's research and post-graduate students come to a total of about two hundred—almost as many as all the undergraduates in some small colleges—and a special tutor has been appointed to look after them. Trinity's financial resources have also made it possible for the college to continue an old Trinity custom and to aid aspects of Cambridge activity lying outside its own gates. It joined Caius and St John's in the establishment of Darwin College, and it has helped New Hall and also the recent women's foundation of Lucy Cavendish College.

No special institutional changes have recently occurred in the College, but one must note the appointment, in 1965, of Lord Butler, a well-known politician of great distinction and also related to a former master, to its mastership. Trinity has also had the privilege of having the heir to the throne as one of its undergraduates. This was not, as with a previous Prince of Wales, and with the present Prince's grandfather, for one year only but for the normal three-year spell of residence. Prince Charles' time at Cambridge was the most normal, and the most successful, experienced by any member of the Royal Family.

Trinity was among the last Colleges to be caught up in Cambridge's great wave of post-war building. The salutary whitening of its chapel choir, and the renovation or modernisation of some of its existing blocks, were for some time more noticeable than totally new work. The old kitchen, well known from one of Ackermann's aquatints, was converted into an attractive dining room, while the repair and redecoration of the Wren library was an outstanding act of historic restoration. Angel Court, squeezed in between Great Court and Trinity Street, was disappointing inside, but admirably preserved the late Georgian frontages on the street's western side. Across the street, an important new development, with the Architects' Co-partnership as its architects, ingeniously serves both commerce and learning. Behind the façade of what was once Matthews' grocer's shop, and between Trinity and Sidney Streets, a large area of jumbled property was gouged out to make way for new buildings. The ground-floor level is shared between Heffer's spacious new book shop (on the Trinity Street side) and a large Sainsbury supermarket. Above the shops an open piazza, paved with dark blue bricks, is approached from the narrow space between Whewell's two courts. Here one finds the new Wolfson Building which gives Trinity about ninety new sets of rooms; the surrounding piazza is more spacious on the Sidney Street side. The appearance of the new block is novel, but its controversial impact is blunted by the fact that little of it can be seen from the streets outside. In the meantime, the scheme for new buildings on a site off Burrell's Walk is in suspense while Trinity reconsiders its needs for in-college accommodation. Some tidying up of the jungle-like site was in progress early in 1973, but this work need not be taken as the prelude to any building operations.

EMMANUEL

THE first of Cambridge's completely post-Reformation Colleges has had a varied and interesting history. It saw a great transformation in its original character, and sharp changes in the religious and social climate signified by the Puritan flavour of its name. Yet its site takes one back to a time earlier than that of any Cambridge college, and to an age when the pre-Reformation teaching of scholastic theology was at its height.

Emmanuel, like most of the colleges in Cambridge's eastern belt, occupies ground which once contained a religious house, or some earlier place of academic education. For its site, since the thirteenth century, had been that of the Dominican friary. Though it passed through several hands in the years soon after the suppression, several of the friars' buildings remained. In the 1580s, the area once used by the Dominicans was still very suitable for the establishment of Cambridge's next academic college.

Emmanuel's founder and its first Master were both Christ's men, and the internal history of Christ's was not without its bearing on the foundation of Emmanuel. Sir Walter Mildmay, the college's Calvinist and Puritan founder, was a typical, highly placed Crown servant of the Tudor age. His father, an Essex gentleman, had been an important, well-enriched official of the Court of Augmentations which had handled the revenues of the dissolved monasteries. Walter Mildmay himself had worked in the Augmentations office, was knighted in his thirties and was still, despite his known religious convictions, employed under Mary I. In the reign of Elizabeth I, he held some important financial posts, including the Chancellorship of the Exchequer, became Walsingham's brother-in-law and a friend of Burghley, and settled down as a landed gentleman in Northamptonshire. He strongly supported the Puritans, while his educational activities included a governorship of Chelmsford School and benefactions to Christ's as well as his foundation of Emmanuel.

In 1582 the Fellows of Christ's asked Mildmay for help and advice over the election of a new Master. But the result of the election, and various other aspects of the running of his old college, seem to have displeased Sir Walter, so much so that he decided to found his own Cambridge college as a stronghold of the conformist Puritanism congenial to so prominent a figure at Court. Mildmay's chosen instrument was Laurence Chaderton, a learned Lancashireman whose leanings were towards the Puritanism favoured by Mildmay. So anxious was the founder to have Chaderton as the head of his new college that he is said to have been unwilling to go ahead with his scheme should Chaderton not be available for Emmanuel's first Mastership. It was Chaderton who, in 1583, acted for Mildmay and bought the site, and the two surviving ranges, of the Dominican friary which had stood not far south of his own college; the property was now to house Mildmay's *seminarium* for the turning out of educated clergy for a Reformed Church. The licence for Emmanuel's foundation came in 1584. The Queen added a little to the new college's revenues, and the buildings were first used, a year before the founder's death, in 1588. The Dominicans' church had become the hall and kitchen range. The western range of the friary housed members of the college, while a new southern range had been put up to the designs of Ralph Symons.

Emmanuel's Puritan character was clear from the start, though it was not until the following century that this feature of the college found its full expression. But even in Chaderton's Mastership, it was said that the Prayer Book services were not fully celebrated in the barn-like, Puritanical chapel which had been built, on a north to south alignment, to emphasise Emmanuel's break with the pre-Reformation past. Chaderton himself, having been among those who translated the Authorised Version, resigned in 1622. But he lived for another eighteen years, and when he died, aged 102 or 103, he became, and has remained, the oldest man to have held the headship of any Cambridge college.

From its earliest days, admissions to Emmanuel had been fairly numerous. By the year when Chaderton retired, matriculations had reached a peak of seventy-nine. Next year, though they were fewer, they were the highest in any college of the University. The great Puritan period now set in, soon leading to the time when the Puritan *seminarium* of Mildmay's intentions was Cambridge's leading college. Laudian liturgical reforms had their effect in Emmanuel, as elsewhere in Cambridge. Some of the University's more stalwart Puritans so much disliked the changes in worship and chapel furnishing that they left for America. By the time of the Civil War, over a third of the Cambridge men who had gone to New England were from

Emmanuel. Simon Bradstreet, the first Governor of Massachusetts, was among them. A more famous name, in New England as in the world at large, was that of John Harvard, the young Emmanuel graduate whose benefactions much strengthened and caused the renaming of the first University to get established in England's American colonies.

The Civil War, Cambridge's early occupation by the forces of Parliament, and the changes in the University which came then and under the Commonwealth, gave Emmanuel its great opportunity. In so staunchly Puritan a college nearly all the Fellows supported the new régime and held their posts; the deprivation of William Sancroft made him, however, an important exception. Emmanuel became the leading nursery of Puritan dons available to fill the posts once held by deprived Royalists. No fewer than eleven vacant Masterships went to Emmanuel men, and the college's numbers went up under the Commonwealth. Some of the leading figures among the Cambridge Platonists were Emmanuel men.

But the Restoration reversed the fortunes of many Emmanuel graduates. Several of them lost their livings in the great upheaval of 1662, while in the college itself (whose condition was poor at the time of the Restoration) abrupt change came with the return in 1662, as Master, of William Sancroft. His short spell of office saw a deliberate realignment of his college's character, and this phase of Emmanuel's history would have been the time when Swift's Gulliver was there. Commonwealth Puritanism gave way to a higher Anglicanism, expressed in the college's finest building.

True to the Laudian tradition, Sancroft disliked Emmanuel's existing, unconsecrated chapel, with its gauntly Puritan design and fittings and with its north to south alignment. He decided, before he was called from his Mastership to the Deanery of St Paul's, to give Emmanuel a chapel whose site, whose correct orientation, and whose fine classical idiom would firmly display the college's new régime. The architect, as for the new chapel at Pembroke with its similar politico-religious background, was Christopher Wren. The chapel's site, in the middle of the main court's eastern side and with delightful flanking loggias, was palpably inspired by the chapel at Peterhouse, with its own high-Anglican links with Matthew Wren and John Cosin. The new chapel was finished in 1677, the year in which Sancroft became Archbishop of Canterbury, and at a time when Emmanuel was Cambridge's largest college. The Corinthian splendour of its west end,*

---

* What seems, on the Peterhouse analogy, to be the west wall of the chapel actually masks the middle section of the long galley which stretches across the East side of the court.

and the round arches of its loggias, contrasted sharply with the medieval and Tudor Gothic character still evident in Emmanuel's other buildings.

Cambridge's eighteenth-century decline was as apparent in Emmanuel as in other colleges. The college was in financial trouble, so that when in the early years of George I's reign Ralph Symons' southern range had to be replaced, the full resources for the task were not available. Much money was borrowed, and much was given by the sixth Earl of Westmorland, a direct descendant of the founder through the daughter and heiress of Sir Walter Mildmay's son. Some of the Earl's forebears had been Emmanuel men, so it was fitting that the new block should be known as the Westmorland Building, and that the arms of the Fanes should be put above the Ionic entrance to its central staircase.

The later decades of the eighteenth century saw a revival in Emmanuel's fortunes. By a sharp contrast with its great Puritan days, it was now a Tory, fashionable college. Its elegant image was displayed in the new block, by James Essex, which replaced the Dominicans' western range. The college's main entrance was now made through this unexciting, yet dignified Ionic façade, and Emmanuel joined such colleges as Caius and Corpus in having its main entrance in another position from that which first served its members.

Richard Farmer, a genial friend of the younger Pitt, was largely responsible, as Master of Emmanuel, for his college's rise in popularity and social standing. Its 130 members in 1788 made Emmanuel the third largest college in Cambridge, its finances improved, and in 1813 the college was said to be 'remarkable for its genteel society'. Though Emmanuel had its measures of Victorian reform the college opposed such innovations as Catholic Emancipation and the railway; a more forward move was the foundation, within the college, of the Dixie Professorship of Ecclesiastical History.

A late Victorian fall in numbers was short lived, and Emmanuel soon regained its normal position as one of Cambridge's largest colleges. In 1910 it stood fourth in numbers, this being the time when the novelty of a subway (beneath Emmanuel Street) led to the excellent neo-Baroque court, by Leonard Stokes, which its numbers now obliged the college to build.

In the 1930s, and since the second World War, Emmanuel has kept its place among the larger colleges of Cambridge. Although it has never returned to the full-blown Puritanism of its early decades, Evangelical beliefs have been held by many Emmanuel men, and in the years before 1939 many of the college's members studied theology with a view to taking

Orders. The college's range of other studies has, however, been as wide as one finds in most Cambridge colleges.

In the post-war years, and until his death as Master early in 1966, Edward Welbourne was the leading Emmanuel man, actively concerning himself with all aspects of college life and still, when Master, controlling the college admissions. Individualism and integrity were qualities which he specially sought, and he deliberately admitted a cross-section of many types. In his time, and since his death, Lancashire and Cheshire have been strong areas for Emmanuel's recruitment; so, too, are the East Midlands. No one school has been specially favoured, and as many as 107 were represented in a recent year's entry of 135 men. Scientists are the strongest single element in a college of some 380 undergraduates, with a house in Hills Road, and one close at hand in St. Andrew's Street, set aside for the inevitably increased post-graduate contingent. Emmanuel's medical entry has remained steady, and of fair size. The influence and example of Lord Birkett helped to build up those reading Law, while economics and English are both relatively larger subjects in Emmanuel than they were before 1939. Apart from restoration work on such buildings as the Brick Building and Wren's chapel new buildings and extra living accommodation have inevitably featured largely in Emmanuel's recent story, and the men out in lodgings are now down to between thirty and forty. The most successful of Emmanuel's new buildings are those of South Court which runs out towards the University Arms. Smaller works include a new Master's Lodge, and an attractive block added, above a slope leading down to the river and the boat-houses, on to the earlier building of Barnwell Hostel. The building, once owned by Jesus, had been a nurses' home. The complete hostel, with some thirty-seven sets, now stands as a close neighbour of the new buildings of the 'Cambridge News'; it is the most north-easterly college building in Cambridge.

SIDNEY SUSSEX

ALTHOUGH Sidney is reckoned as an essentially Protestant foundation, with early resemblances between it and the larger, slightly older Elizabethan College of Emmanuel, some points in its earliest history remind one of certain pre-Reformation Cambridge colleges, particularly those which owed their being to pious, highly-connected ladies. Although Pembroke is more like Sidney in that a great lady initiated the entire project, there was also a resemblance, seen by Sidney's foundress, between the second of Cambridge's Elizabethan foundations and the riverside college of Clare Hall.

The foundress of Sidney was Frances, the daughter of Sir Henry Sidney and the aunt of the famous Sir Philip Sidney. Her husband, who died without heirs in 1583, was Thomas Radcliffe, Earl of Sussex. The widowed and childless Countess decided, soon before her own death in 1589, to devote some of her property to the founding, at Cambridge, of another college for the education of future clergy of the Church of England. Though the new foundation was in some ways less markedly Puritan than Emmanuel, Sir Walter Mildmay's college served as a model for Sidney Sussex. Sidney's first statutes were based on those of Emmanuel, the word *seminarium* was used, as it was with Emmanuel, to describe it, and the profession of the 'pure', i.e. strictly Reformed, religion, and opposition both to 'Popery' and 'other heresies' were provided for in the new college's constitution. More crucial, at the time of Sidney's inception, were the conditions of finance under which the Countess's executors had to set about their task.

Sidney Sussex resembled St John's in that its foundress died before its establishment was really begun. The Countess's executors, and in particular her nephew, Sir John Harington, of Exton, Rutland, did for this small new college what Fisher had done for the second of the Lady Margaret Beaufort's two Cambridge colleges. The successful establishment of Sidney might never, however, have come about.

The sum set aside by the Countess for the founding of her new college came to £5,000; some plate and other goods were also available. Lady Frances had directed that, if her money was inadequate for the founding of a new college, it was to go to the augmentation of Clare; one sees, in her choice of an alternative, a deliberate reminiscence of Lady Clare in the fourteenth century. But her executors decided, in the end at much personal cost to themselves, to go ahead with the scheme for a new place of education. Clare lost its chance both of an increase in its income and of a renaming which would, on the analogy of Gonville and Caius, have given it the cumbrous title of 'Clare and Lady Frances Sidney Sussex College or Hall'.

The site earmarked for the new college was the convenient one long occupied by Cambridge's Franciscan Friary. It was bounded on one side by the stagnant channel of the King's Ditch, which still formed an eastern edge to the urban area. Since 1546 the site had been Trinity property, and as the friars' church and most of their domestic buildings had been carried away as building materials the site was less well equipped for college purposes than that of the Dominicans had been for Emmanuel.

There was moreover some difficulty with Trinity whose authorities were unwilling to sell the site, and Elizabeth I herself had to apply pressure before they would comply. Though the Countess's executors had got a licence, in 1594, to found the new college another year passed before building work could start on the conversion (into a chapel and library block) of the one remaining Franciscan building, and on the building of Ralph Symons' attractive brick and stone court which at first gave Sidney most of its accommodation.

Harington and the Earl of Kent had been assiduous, and personally generous, in carrying out the Countess's intentions, the formal foundation of Sidney came in 1596, and the buildings were first used in 1598. The new college, which has never been large or really wealthy, started with its members far fewer than those intended by the foundress. Benefactions from other well-wishers soon increased them, and Fellow Commoners, 'of virtuous life and unsullied reputation' might also be admitted; it was under this heading that Sidney soon entered its most famous member.

Sidney's first Master was well suited to the task of setting the little college on its way. He was Dr James Montagu, a relative both of Sir John Harington and of the foundress, a Christ's man and later best known as the Bishop of Bath and Wells who completed the building of Bath Abbey, which now contains his splendid tomb. He actively recruited both Fellows and junior members, while among the physical improvements which he brought about was the leading into Cambridge, from just below the Gogs, of the artificial waterway now known as Hobson's Conduit. One of the new channel's purposes was to stir up and sweeten the noisome water of the King's Ditch where it intersected the garden of Sidney, and James Montagu deserved at least as much credit as did Hobson the carrier for one of Cambridge's most famous 'improvements'.

For many years, and to its great advantage, Sidney became the favoured college of the important Montagu family. James Montagu gave up his mastership in 1608. In 1616, quite early in the long mastership of Samuel Ward, the young Oliver Cromwell entered Sidney as a Fellow Commoner; his family's friendship with the Montagues may well have been the cause of his entry into Sidney. But as his father died in 1617, the future Lord Protector left Sidney at the end of his first year, too soon for him to have made any mark in his undergraduate career.

Though Sidney grew quickly in the early Stuart period, and though it maintained a largely Puritan character, it was less important than Emmanuel as a nursery of Puritan replacements for the numerous Masters and Fellows who lost their posts in Cambridge in and after 1643. The Earl of Manchester, who carried out Parliament's orders for the 'regulation' of the University, was one of the Montagues who had been at Sidney. But he showed no special favour to his old college, and that same year saw the imprisonment, and swift death, of the Puritan, yet firmly Royalist Master Samuel Ward. The Restoration period, not a good one for Sidney and a time of financial difficulties and indifferent discipline, coincided with the long Mastership, for over forty years from 1643, of Dr Richard Minshull.

Then there followed one of the dramatic episodes in Sidney's history, a Cambridge equivalent to James II's famous, and tactless proceedings at Magdalen, Oxford. For Joshua Basset, a Roman Catholic priest, was made Master of Sidney, by royal mandate and against the College Statutes and the Fellows' wishes. Basset soon opened the way to the admission of Catholic Fellows and junior members, and he had Mass said, in a room fitted up as a chapel, in the Master's Lodge.

The fall of James II soon ended Basset's short mastership, and Sidney then settled down to a placid, undistinguished spell which covered most of the eighteenth century. The college's income was modest and Fellowships were often left open so that their revenues could pay for the fair amount of building and furnishing work which still went on. The hall was thus converted, about 1750, into a particularly fine Georgian interior, while between

EMMANUEL. The Brick Building by John Westley, 1634

SIDNEY SUSSEX. The Gate Tower and Chapel court

DOWNING. A Garden Scene, 'Contemporary' and Grecian

1776 and 1782 a small, simple new chapel by James Essex replaced the converted refrectory of the Franciscans. More important, for the balance of studies in a college which had so far been almost wholly theological, a bequest of 1723 by Samuel Taylor of Dudley in the Black Country provided for a mathematical Fellow and led, as the value of the Dudley property increased with the Industrial Revolution, to the growth of a strong mathematical tradition in Sidney. All through the eighteenth century the college's entries were few, those resident in Sidney (seniors and juniors together) seldom if ever going above the modest number of forty.

Regency Sidney saw a series of short masterships before the long spell in office of Dr William Chafy. In his time the genuinely Elizabethan appearance of Sidney was much changed by the architect, Sir Jeffrey Wyattville. He used a coating of Roman cement to give a stonework appearance to his pseudo-Elizabethan style. He also gave the college its excellent main entrance, at the street end of the central range, which parts its two original courts. Dr Chafy himself was twice Vice-Chancellor, and Sidney became the scene of elaborate social occasions untypical of most of its comparatively quiet history.

The range of its studies continued to widen. Science and mathematics were notably strong, and Sidney became the first Cambridge college to build its own laboratory. For a time it remained very small, at times with fewer than a dozen undergraduate members. But later, in the Victorian period, the development of its Lincolnshire property near Cleethorpes increased the income, the numbers, and the buildings of the college. Then the early years of the present century saw a marked change in Sidney's religious emphasis; its enlarged and wholly transformed chapel became, for several years, the scene of 'higher' services than those held in other Cambridge colleges.

Sidney's buildings were much increased in the years between the wars, with Sidney a pioneer, in the neo-Georgian transformation of Sussex Street, in the process whereby urban development also caused an increase in college accommodation. Sidney grew, but was still smaller than most other colleges in Cambridge, with an emphasis on steady academic study rather than any great reputation as a sporting or 'social' college. Numbers fell, as they did elsewhere in Cambridge, during the first World War. But after 1918 they rose sharply, so that the new buildings South and East of the two original courts proved useful to house the influx.

New buildings, and the repair and renovation of those already existing, have also figured large in Sidney's recent history. The latest block, by the London architects Howell, Killick, Partridge and Amis, is sited towards the corner of King and Malcolm Streets. It provides many rooms for undergraduates as well as some sets for Fellows. The architects have cleverly used a restricted, difficult site, but the tints of their brickwork are somewhat sombre, and the corridors inside the building are decidedly dark. Garages have been provided under one side of the new building, and in the yard towards King Street.

Sidney's undergraduates now number about 240, with mathematics, science, and engineering in their well-established position of strength. There has, however, been no drastic change in the proportion of Sidney men reading the subjects now studied at Cambridge. English and geography are, however, on the increase, as they are in several other colleges. As Sidney now supports more Fellows, it can now offer tuition, from its own resources, in more subjects than it has ever done since its exclusively theological late Tudor days.

DOWNING

HAD the will of the third Sir George Downing been carried out soon after his death there would still have been a gap of over a century and a half between the commencement of his college and the last previous foundation in Cambridge. Any college thus started might also have been similar, in its staffing and teaching, to those already on the scene. But the actual interval between the foundation of Sidney and the first building work done at Downing was well over two hundred years, and Downing College turned out very different, both in its constitution and its buildings, from the other foundations so far made in Cambridge.

The early history of Downing was not only unusual for the long delay which elapsed between the founder's death and the actual starting of his college. The relationship between Downing College and Sir George was more distant than that of any Cambridge college with its founder, while one has also to admit that the third baronet himself, of a family also known for its ownership of the site duly occupied by the Premier's official residence, was probably the least admirable character among those who have set a Cambridge college on its way. About the most pleasing thing that Downing College has taken from its founder is its heraldry, for to my mind the coat of arms of the college which in the end was built in Pembroke Leys is at least as attractive as any college coat in Cambridge.

The Downings took their origin from the eastern counties. They had a Cambridge background, including links with Queens', Clare and St John's, as well as the interesting historical point that the first baronet was Harvard's second graduate and was later on the staff of the famous Massachusetts College.

The second Sir George was a reprobate, who underwent excommunication and treated his wife so badly that the lady died as a result. The third baronet, by whose will the college came into being, lived apart from his father; his unhappy childhood may partly explain his own unstable and unsatisfactory life. When only fifteen he married his thirteen-year-old cousin, but never lived with his wife. Her failure, in 1715, to get a Bill of Divorce was the prelude, in 1717, to the making of Sir George's will whose academic fruits were not really apparent until 1807.

Though Sir George's Cambridge background may have given him some interest in education the creation of a new college could hardly have seemed likely when he planned the disposal of his large estates. For four cousins had to die, and leave no issue, before the property and its income could be used for the foundation of the college for whose academic character the thirty-three-year-old founder made no special provision. The eventual existence of Downing College came as a reminder of the hazards of life among the Georgian gentry. Sir George Downing died in 1749, in his country house at Gamlingay in the extreme west of Cambridgeshire. Sir Jacob Garrard Downing, the cousin first named as his heir, died childless in 1764. By then all the other three heirs had also died childless. The foundation of Downing College should now have gone ahead. But Sir Jacob's widow seems at once to have made it clear that she meant to keep the estates. So the University started a suit in Chancery, and in five years got a judgment in its favour. But Sir Jacob's widow, who had now remarried, proved tenacious, bequeathing the estates to relatives and remaining in possession until her own death in 1778. Costly litigation went on for over twenty years more, and it was not until 1800 that Downing College's Royal Charter was obtained.

By the time that Downing College got its Charter several sites for its buildings had been considered, and some provisional designs had been made. The years of litigation had used up much of the money left at the time of Sir Jacob's death, and the new foundation suffered severely, the more so because its estates had been much neglected and brought in less than they should have done. The superb designs eventually approved for its buildings thus proved far too ambitious for the money available. But the scheme got out for the new college was of a challenging novelty, more in tune with the Age of Enlightenment than with the early Hanoverian years when Sir George Downing had made his will.

Sir George had laid it down that the foundation process should be super-vised by the Archbishops of Canterbury and York, and by the Masters of St John's and Clare. But it is said that a strong eventual influence was that of the younger Pitt and that to him the novel, and mainly lay, character of the new college was largely due. Only two of the Fellows were to be in

Orders, various reforming points were to be included into the statutes, and the endowments provided for Professors of Law and Medicine whose lectures were to be open to anyone in the University. Official houses were to be provided for these professors in the splendid ensemble of buildings planned for Downing. The architect chosen, after several others had been considered, was William Wilkins, then in the wholly Grecian phase of his career. The college's spacious site, then about double what it is now, gave Cambridge an opportunity for monumental collegiate planning such as it had not seen since Henry VI made his plans for King's. Wilkins's designs, in the purest Greek style, were worthy of so great a chance; had they been fully carried out they would have given Cambridge its equivalent to the Grecian monumentality of Munich, Edinburgh, Berlin and Plymouth.

What Wilkins designed for Downing had all the components now normal for a college. But the main buildings were to be detached from each other, and Wilkins's grouping was a pioneering version of an American campus rather than the tighter enclosure of a traditional 'Oxbridge' quad or court. The splendid, unbuilt southern range was closely akin to the architect's simultaneously designed main block at the East India Company's College at Haileybury, but in general Downing had more of the spirit of the monumentally laid out 'academical village' which Thomas Jefferson built, at Charlottesville, for the University of Virginia. To the north of the site a splendid, very Athenian, propylaeum was to look out towards what is now Downing Street. Cambridge was vastly impressed with the classical poise and monumental quality of the scheme. Even when partly built it became the University's great showpiece, and the author Maria Edgeworth regretfully found herself not 'with it' when she could not think Downing College equal to King's chapel.

Work started in 1807. Money was short, progress was slow, and in 1811 the college's only resident was Sir Busick Harwood, its first Professor of Medicine; when in another three years he died he was buried within the site earmarked for the chapel. Francis Annesley, the first Master, was a distant relative of the founder and had long held the headship of the uncommenced college. His Lodge was one of the early buildings and as the Hall was finished in 1821 the first undergraduates could then be admitted. The first Professor of Law was Edward Christian, a brother of Fletcher Christian, the leader of the 'Bounty's' mutineers and at the time of that famous voyage the University's counsel against the embattled heirs of the Downings. His nineteenth-century successors included W. Lloyd Birkbeck and the very eminent F. W. Maitland.

For financial and other reasons, Downing was slow to develop along normal college lines. Its building scheme was too ambitious for the money available, and on two occasions Fellowships had to be reduced below the sixteen normally allowed for. Entries were few for several years, and of those who did come many were Fellow Commoners, some being older men than was normal among Cambridge undergraduates. Some well-known people were, however, associated with the new college. J. M. Neale, the prominent Tractarian clergyman, lectured there for a short time. C. S. Kenny, the great exponent of the law, was a Downing man; so, too, was Philip Schreiner, who was Prime Minister of Cape Colony when the South African War broke out.

Of the mid-Victorian Presidents of the Union a remarkably high proportion came from Downing, while the college's range of studies widened out a little beyond medicine and law. But the buildings were never finished as Wilkins planned them, and during the late Victorian years of agricultural depression Downing lost heavily on its none-too-fertile West Cambridgeshire estates. So bad did its position become that it had to sell to the University the northern half of its site, now filled by scientific and other buildings to the south of Downing Street and also a strip of ground, along part of Lensfield Road, now covered by a row of late Victorian houses. Shortly before 1900 Downing's undergraduate membership averaged no more than twenty or thirty, and the remaining Fellow Commoners, along with some Indians from wealthy families, helped to swell the college's finances.

From about 1900, under the wise guidance of Henry Jackson and J. H. Widdicombe, great changes came over Downing. Its numbers started to rise and by 1914 the college had over one hundred undergraduates, with a somewhat wider range of subjects read, and agricultural science pursued with marked success. The college had, moreover, gained a 'reading' reputation. Its whole evolution in this century has been one of closer assimilation to the other colleges of Cambridge which are themselves much altered and reformed, since Victorian times, in the direction originally marked out for Downing itself.

Downing's progress, academically and in other fields, continued after the first World War; by 1930 its undergraduates numbered some 150, with about 200 not long before 1939. New buildings, by Sir Herbert Baker and in a Georgian idiom rather earlier than that of Wilkins, were added near the northern end of the much-diminished site. The gap between those two blocks has now been filled by a range whose central element, behind a six-columned portico, is a chapel of the normal collegiate type.

Downing has not lacked its leading personalities in modern times. Dr F. R. Leavis, by origin an Emmanuel man, was long a Fellow, and then an

Honorary Fellow, of Downing. The late Sir Lionel Whitby, of great distinction as a pathologist and the reorganiser of the Cambridge Medical School, was a Downing alumnus as well as being the college's Master, while his predecessor Vice-Admiral Sir Herbert Richmond was a notably popular social figure in Cambridge and was the first Admiral ever to attain a college headship.

Since the war Downing has gone still further in its integration into the University as a whole. For financial and other reasons, its undergraduate numbers have again risen, being a little over three hundred at present. Downing's post-graduate and research students are so far fewer, in relation to the college's total strength, than in most other colleges, but its Fellows now exceed two dozen and offer widely ranging college tuition.

The Kenny Court, built in two stages in the 'Regency' vein traditional in Downing, was a further move in the college's policy of housing as many as possible of its members. But in its most recent development, with Howell, Killick, Partridge, and Amis as the architects, Downing has moved over to a more 'contemporary' phase. The new, detached Senior Combination Room block has something of the feeling, in a highly modern idiom, of a delicate little Chinese tea house which could have been an ornament to a mid-eighteenth-century college had Downing been built within a few years of its founder's death.

FITZWILLIAM

FITZWILLIAM at Cambridge, and St Catherine's at Oxford, owe their existence to the reform movement which in the last century spread gradually over both of England's ancient Universities. Their story proves how dominant the collegiate idea had become by the time they set out on their academic and social course.

The Royal Commission on Oxford and Cambridge was appointed in 1850 and reported in 1852. One of its recommendations was that the two Universities should go back to their original practice and admit students who would not belong to any college. This, it was felt, would make for a University education within the means of many who could not, at that time afford to come up as pensioners. The Commissioners (and here one senses the hidden influence of the Prince Consort who had studied at Bonn) were impressed by the non-collegiate system which prevailed in the Universities of Germany.

This recommendation was far better received at Oxford than it was in Cambridge. Even so, things moved slowly in both places, and in 1867 Parliament threw out a Bill which aimed at the creation, in both Universities, of non-collegiate societies; its opponents made much of the inferior social position which such bodies would have and stressed their probable lack of the self-respect and *esprit de corps* which went with the fully developed college system. Yet a few non-collegiate students did gain admission both to Oxford and Cambridge, and in 1868 Oxford allowed the matriculation of men who were *nulli collegio vel aulae adscripti*. Cambridge followed suit next year, so 1969 saw the centenary of what was at first, unromantically, known as the Non-Collegiate Students' Board. The Vice-Chancellor was the head of the newly created body, while the title of Censor was given to the senior member of the University who performed the duties of a Tutor.

The first Censor was a Trinity man, the Rev. Ralph Benjamin Somerset. His office was in a room in the building until recently known as Fitzwilliam House, and all that the students had to do there was to report five days a week, and occasionally to send the Censor a written report on the progress of their studies. Corporate life, for the moment, was wholly lacking. But Mr Somerset encouraged it, and to give the little society a better standing in Cambridge he strongly urged that it should have the use of some building belonging to the University itself.

It might have seemed, back in 1869 and for the next few years, that Cambridge had returned, in a small-scale way, to the days when membership of a college was in no way essential to membership of the University. After all, non-collegiate students had once been the overwhelming majority of those up at Oxford and Cambridge. But things had changed much by 1869. The colleges had become dominant and could offer strong inducements to the best of those who had started their University career elsewhere.

The history of Cambridge's non-collegiate students has been one of assimilation to college life, leading on to the coming of fully collegiate status. The college system, immensely strong after nearly seven centuries of growth and acceptance, has remained the triumphant essence of Cambridge's academic life.

The original non-collegiate body at Cambridge was a good deal smaller than its Oxford counterpart which got considerable encouragement, and fairly generous financial aid, from the University. By the end of its first academic year, nineteen residents had kept the third term. The students were encouraged to meet and to form clubs, and in 1874 some rooms for those meetings were hired in the building which already contained the Censor's office. This house had been built, in 1727, by the Halsteads who were a local brewing family; it is an excellent specimen of the early Georgian Cambridge town house. When the non-collegiate body first used part of it the house was known as 31 Trumpington Street; some years passed before it gained the name later passed on to the fully fledged Fitzwilliam College.

Sporting clubs apart, a small library and a common room were soon provided in the Trumpington Street house. The men remained, however, in lodgings, and their social life was much less closely knit than in the colleges. Many of the best non-collegiate men migrated, and in some years the new society's losses to the well-established colleges were as much as a third, or even half.

But things slowly improved, especially after the Non-Collegiate Board bought Halstead House, reorganised it inside, and in 1892 reopened it as a larger, better equipped headquarters than the University's non-collegiate element had so far been able to use. They sought a title more distinctive than a number in Trumpington Street, and as their fine Georgian headquarters stood opposite the Fitzwilliam Museum they called the house Fitzwilliam Hall. The then Earl Fitzwilliam kindly allowed the society to use his arms in a coat which included, in chief, those of the University. But one has to remember that this Fitzwilliam name comes solely from the geographical nearness of Halstead House to the Museum. Had the Museum been sited elsewhere (as it might well have been), or had the Non-Collegiate Board fixed its headquarters in some other building, the name of the present Fitzwilliam College would not have been what it is.

From the time of its naming, and from the complete occupation of the house in Trumpington Street, Fitzwilliam Hall moved forward in the development of its corporate life. Though it little resembled what people now accepted as a normal college, the warmth and intensity of that corporate life was little affected during the decades when Fitzwilliam men made do with their home opposite the great classical museum. One could, indeed, claim that the very difficulties which beset the comparatively new society helped on a specially devoted collegiate feeling. Things were much assisted when in 1907, Mr W. F. Reddaway, of King's, was appointed Censor. Migrations to other colleges sharply dropped, dining in hall became normal, a chapel was fitted out, and a hostel was provided for the lodging of some Fitzwilliam men.

Fitzwilliam Hall shared fully in the University's great expansion soon after the end of the first World War. Some nearby houses were bought to provide hostel accommodation for some of the numerous Fitzwilliam men, and the first moves were now made towards the society's status as an independent college. But a check soon came, the non-collegiate status of Fitzwilliam still being thought helpful in providing an inexpensive university education for those who could not afford the colleges.

Despite some improved provisions for its corporate life Fitzwilliam's numbers temporarily fell, with its membership reaching a low point of 147 men in 1926. But the change, in 1934, of its title to Fitzwilliam House, and the ending of the term 'non-collegiate' for its members, suggested that an advance to full collegiate rank might not be far away. Despite the cramped, uncollegiate nature of its Georgian house, the main aspects of college life were pursued there, on the river, and on the playing fields. A few Fitzwilliam men were older than the normal undergraduate age, while between the wars men from Fitzwilliam were relatively more numerous in Fitzwilliam than in some of the colleges.

The second World War caused the complete, though temporary, fading out of Fitzwilliam. But as soon as it ended there was an astonishingly swift rebirth. With more than 400 students in 1950 Fitzwilliam found itself the fifth largest society in the University; among its members more than 100 research students were a foretaste of the great wave which has swept over Cambridge in the post-war years. It was a pioneering move, again foreshadowing what has since happened almost everywhere else in Cambridge, when these post-graduates at Fitzwilliam were given a club room of their own. Ninety of those who were on Fitzwilliam's books in 1950 came from overseas, twenty-eight countries being represented.

Since 1952 the history of Fitzwilliam has largely consisted of the gradual yet final stages by which it attained the full status of a college. That year the Regent House approved a policy whereby the corporate life of the revived, much enlarged Fitzwilliam House should be encouraged, with its continuance on the basis of a membership of 400 or more made possible by the erection of new, larger, and properly collegiate buildings. A fund was started, considerable sums were raised by Fitzwilliam men, and King's contributed handsomely in memory of W. F. Reddaway. It proved essential, however, for the University to bear most of the necessary capital cost, and it found itself able to provide money at first earmarked for other projects which have so far failed to reach fruition.

By 1960 the site for the new college, lying between Huntingdon Road and Storey's Way, had been found and Mr Denys Lasdun was preparing his plans, working outwards, as in a helical movement but with angled corners, from the central, most communal building which contained the hall, the library, and the combination rooms. Work soon started, and by the middle of 1963 the first buildings, in their unquestioningly 'contemporary' style, with their fine display of brickwork, and with their study bedrooms restricted to the modest size laid down by the University Grants Committee, were finished and in use. Fitzwilliam men, now far too many for them to live a contented college life in the Trumpington Street house, and with a wide range both of sporting, academic and social pursuits, that could now be sure they had headquarters more obviously suited to their modern needs.

The University authorities were now satisfied that the new buildings, and the society's endowed income coming in from the money subscribed, justified the seeking of an independent college status. The final phase of the non-collegiate body's evolution now set in. A charter was granted on 10 September 1966, and the full status of a college followed next day.

Since the move to the new buildings, Fitzwilliam men have increased in numbers, and the college's undergraduate figure of about 450 is the third largest in Cambridge. The buildings themselves have been enlarged, though Mr Lasdun's full plan is not yet complete. About half of the college's men live in, and Fitzwilliam's corporate life, though perhaps no stronger than in the more difficult years when it was a struggle to keep it going in any form, is full of vigour.

The college's athletic successes were considerable, and three of 1968's winning Boat Race crew were Fitzwilliam men. Post-graduate and research students make up a high proportion of Fitzwilliam's members, and the college's undergraduates read a wide range of subjects. A recent move is the attachment to Fitzwilliam as affiliated students of some of the men studying in Cambridge's various theological colleges. Occasional dining in Hall symbolises the connection of these men with the society which has now after nearly a century won through to the status which seemed very remote in the first days of the Non-Collegiate Students' Board.

CAVENDISH

WHATEVER may have happened in the days when 'poor scholars' came readily to the schools at Cambridge, or entered the colleges as scholars or sizars, by the mid-Victorian period an Oxford or Cambridge education was hard to obtain unless one had at least a reasonable income. Many colleges had become the increasingly exclusive preserves of those with money or high birth. Some of the moves which were made, in the middle decades of the last century, to reform the University and the colleges, and to widen their scope, were concerned with the problems of lower middle class students.

It was still almost unthinkable, as Hardy pointed out in 'Jude the Obscure', that 'Oxbridge' should be open to the sons of manual workers. But the non-collegiate system and the creation of some other academic organisations did do something for the sons of the less affluent professional men. A landmark of some importance was the establishment, largely for intending schoolmasters who came from such homes, of what came to be known as Cavendish College.

The founding of Cavendish was part of a wider mid-Victorian move to extend and indeed to make universal the country's system of education, and to make it possible for the Universities to draw recruits from a wider social field than that which had become normal by about 1870. It was, in particular, closely linked to the efforts of the County Colleges Association. This body was under the guidance of the Rev. Joseph Lloyd Brereton, the Rector of West Buckland in North Devon and the founder there in 1858 of a 'County School' for the sons of farmers. Brereton was much assisted by his near neighbour the fourth Earl Fortescue, who did much, in Devon and elsewhere, for educational reform.

The association had come into being to assist in the creation, for the sons of farmers and professional men, of 'County Colleges' which would give higher education, particularly to would-be teachers. Lord Fortescue hoped for such a college in his own county. But no Devonshire University was started in Victorian times. It was in Cambridge, in Cavendish College, that the work of the County Colleges Association bore short-lived fruit. The story of the college is one of a gradual evolution, from beginnings which made it unlike the colleges of the University, to a status close to that of the colleges which existed by 1890.

From 1867 Brereton was rector of what had been his father's parish of Little Massingham, near King's Lynn. One can, in a way, liken him to that other Norfolk parson, Edmund Gonville, who founded a college in Cambridge. From Devon he now turned his attention to the two ancient Universities. His efforts to found a County College at Oxford (his own University) were a failure. But Cambridge proved more favourable. The County Colleges' plans to found an establishment on what was then the outer edge of Cambridge must have been made in the first half of the 1870s, for Francis Lloyd Brereton, a son of the Rector of Little Massingham, was entered on the books of 'Cavendish Hostel' in 1873. But the real year of the college's foundation was 1876, and the founder's ideas were clear in the speeches made when the foundation stone of the first new buildings (by John Giles of Cambridge) was laid in October of that year.

The name of the new college came from the Duke of Devonshire, who in his long and active Chancellorship of the University laid the foundation stone. T. J. Lawrence was the first Warden, and the first Trustees and Directors included Lord Fortescue, the Bishop of Winchester (who had earlier been at Ely), the Speaker of the House of Commons, the then Master of Trinity, and Ebenezer Bird Foster, a member of the local family who ran Foster's Bank, which numbered many Cambridgeshire farmers among its customers. The Foster family were important among the college's supporters and benefactors.

Another leading Governor and benefactor, well known for the wide range of his educational and philanthropic work, was Samuel Morley, a prominent M.P. and a Nonconformist who had, for religious reasons, been denied a University education. It was a reflection of his views that Cavendish, described as 'neither a Godless College nor a mere training college for schoolmasters', was undenominational.

The Cavendish students, most of them entering at sixteen or seventeen, were to be rather younger than the undergraduates in the actual University. Most of them were expected to get degrees, and to become full members of the University, but those not intending to do so would none the less be admitted. Those wishing to become schoolmasters would get 'training in the art of teaching'. All Cavendish men were to come up for four terms a year, the terms themselves being of ten weeks instead of eight, the fourth of them being the 'long vac' term.

The fees at Cavendish were to be low, with somewhat Spartan standards to go with them, and Cavendish men were to have the 'advantages of a wise economy' both of time and money. But the college's promoters did not wish it to be 'a mere class institution', or to lower the value of a Cambridge degree by conferring it indiscriminately on 'a mob of raw boys'. Nor did they wish to make it 'a sort of moral hot house for forcing a crop of sickly virtues from youth kept carefully unexposed to the atmosphere of the outside world'.

The new college started modestly, and the first Cavendish men came under the scope of the Non-Collegiate Students' Board which later became Fitzwilliam House. The University Almanac of 1879 said that twenty-nine students were then in residence; John Cox had by that time succeeded Lawrence as Warden. Further expansion, in a wholly residential college, had to await the gradual completion of the buildings which still bear the arms of the Cavendishes and of Brereton. By the end of 1879 there were sixty-one students, another block to hold thirty-four was soon to be ready and the ultimate plan was to run up to 300.

The Warden's Report of 1880 recorded further progress, and mentioned the boat which had been jointly given to the college Rowing Club by the Duke of Devonshire and Samuel Morley. This boat had gone up three places that year, and by 1882 it was nearly top of the Second Division. A reminder of Cavendish College's prowess on the river is an oar of the 1882 boat, with the college arms which were those of the Devonshires, which still hangs in a hall of what is now Homerton College.

The year 1882 saw the recognition of Cavendish College as a Public Hostel in the University. From then onwards its members were no longer supervised by the Non-Collegiate Students' Board. Its prospects seemed reasonably bright, despite the out-of-town isolation of its site in a virtually bicycle-free Cambridge whose horse-drawn tram service (from the Station and along the upper part of Hills Road) was limited to a pace of three miles an hour. The founder's son, who had been Cavendish's first entrant, was a lecturer there from 1879 to 1883.

In 1886 the college was ten years old and there had been real if limited progress. Migrations to other colleges had ceased, for a time, when Cavendish got its recognition as a Public Hostel. But the cramped discomfort of the students' single rooms was a disadvantage only partly mitigated by the allowance, to third-year men, of a keeping room as well as a bedroom. When the shortage of buildings led to the withdrawal of that privilege, migrations started again. The Warden, in his report of 1886, recommended that the second room should again be allowed. He also criticised the kitchens as they then existed, also the lack of a properly collegiate hall, of a specially built chapel, and of a library—buildings which in other colleges aroused 'a sense of dignity and pride' and helped to create *esprit de corps*.

Matriculations in the past four years had averaged thirty-six a year, and 281 men (some the sons of clergy and sixty-four from business families) had so far entered Cavendish. By the end of the same year, ninety-nine had graduated, twenty-seven of them with honours.

Cavendish's tenth anniversary seemed a good opportunity for a serious effort to complete the college buildings as originally envisaged. The Duke of Devonshire, as the largest shareholder, encouraged his colleagues to raise extra money; he and G. E. Foster each gave £5,000 for the building of the new central block now put in hand. A new Governing Body was also formed to take over from the now defunct County Colleges Association. The Duke of Devonshire was President of the new College Council and three members, among them the Master of Christ's and C. S. Kenny of Downing, were appointed by the Council of the University Senate. J. H. Flather, an Emmanuel man who had been Tutor of the College, was appointed as the first and, as it happened, the only Master of Cavendish.

The main event of 1889 was the building of the hall, designed by Giles and Gough, pronouncedly Gothic, and with the unusual feature of a rose window. It is a spacious building, and ranks among the largest college halls in Cambridge. A tower planned for one side of it was never built, nor was the proposed chapel-cum-divinity school whose tower, octagonal lantern, and tall spire would have comprised one of Cambridge's most ambitious Victorian buildings. For despite the new régime, and the money put into the venture by the Duke and the Fosters, Cavendish College was now in its final decline. Its finances were precarious, its living conditions were still somewhat unattractive, and it now suffered from the competition of Selwyn, which was preferred by many Anglican clergy who wanted an economical Cambridge education for their sons.

Early in 1891 an appeal for their support was made to businessmen. It was explained that a Cavendish man, after his early entry, could take a degree, and be ready for a technical career, by the age of twenty. But all efforts to revive the college's fortunes were in vain. In October of 1891 the College Council decided, to meet the wishes of its students and of their parents, to close Cavendish at the end of the year. All the students were given leave to migrate. Some of them, and some of the college's graduates, went to Downing or became non-collegiate.

The Cavendish buildings stayed empty for a few years, but new life came to them in 1894 when they were taken over by Homerton College. This was a training college for men and women teacher trainees, established at Homerton in North London and virtually refounded, under the guidance of Samuel Morley, on the site which it now vacated. Though Morley had died in 1886, one may think of him as an important link between the Cavendish and Homerton phases of the history of these buildings down Hills Road. Soon after its coming to Cambridge, Homerton confined itself to the training of women. Many additions have been made, since then, to the buildings, but the Cavendish oar, the Devonshire and Brereton coats of arms, and some hall tables with their lettering CAV. COLL., can still remind Homerton's present residents of a gallant academic failure in Victorian Cambridge.

SELWYN

THE setting up of the Non-Collegiate Students' Board, and the foundation of the short-lived Cavendish College, were two stages in the mid-Victorian movement to make a Cambridge education more accessible to men who were at some social or financial disadvantage compared to most of those who found their way to the two ancient Universities.

The 1870s saw the first moves towards the founding of another college whose task was in some ways like that which lay before Cavendish College and what eventually became Fitzwilliam House. The new college did not, however, come into being for the sole purpose of reducing the expenses of more parents who wished to send their sons to Cambridge. It also had a specifically religious and, in fact, Church of England background, and its history shows that many Anglican clergymen have sent their sons there. So far as Cambridge may be said to have an opposite number to Keble College at Oxford this could be found on a site which once formed part of Corpus Christi College's holding in what was long the open agricultural space of Cambridge Field. Selwyn College was founded to commemorate Bishop Selwyn of New Zealand, and later of Lichfield, who died in 1878; the arms of the Bishop's English see are those which appear in those of the college.

Selwyn College in its early days had to be seen not only as a memorial to an eminent Cambridge churchman but as a weapon in the counter-attack being made on the religious 'broadening out' of a University whose long-standing Anglican character seemed, to some, to be endangered by such changes as the abolition of denominational tests for all but the heads of colleges and those who sat for degrees in divinity.

It was in the year of Bishop Selwyn's death that a specially formed committee made plans for a new college to bear his name. The bishop had been one of the founders of Keble, so it was appropriate, and to be expected, that the Constitution of Selwyn was based on that of Keble, and that its Charter of 1882 reproduced many points from Keble's equivalent document. By that year the entrance range of Arthur Blomfield's buildings, in the early Tudor style then so much in vogue for educational buildings, had been started, and a temporary hall and chapel were used for the college's first few years. The buildings were simple and unluxurious and stress was laid, in Selwyn, on plain living standards combined with good cultural attainments and a definitely Christian corporate life based on Church of England principles. Yet despite the strongly Anglican stamp of Selwyn College its undergraduates, as distinct from its first scholars and senior members, were not obliged to be members of the Church of England. But few Selwyn men who came up before 1914 were not Anglicans, and Selwyn long had a more distinctively Anglican (though not necessarily High Anglican) character than other colleges in Cambridge.

Selwyn's status was not that of the older established colleges. It was not fully incorporated into the University, but in 1883 Selwyn, like Cavendish, was accorded the newly recognised position of a Public Hostel; it remained, till 1926, in this first stage towards the acknowledgment of its full collegiate standing. Under these initial arrangements its Masters could not nominate proctors or hold the vice-chancellorship, and till as late as 1936 all its undergraduates were obliged to live in college. Selwyn's senior members at first had the title not of Fellows but of Lecturers, and it was only in 1913 that they took over the running of the college from the council which had been formed at its foundation and which had, till then, administered the college.

The rate of Selwyn's growth was much tied up with the speed with which its first buildings were put up. It started with twenty-eight undergraduates and had over fifty in the second year of its career. Progress was reasonably swift and the chapel, aligned to the court as are those of Peterhouse and Emmanuel, was built in the 1890s. The sons of clergy were, as we have seen, very numerous among Selwyn men, and many of those who came to the college took Anglican orders. An important event in the first years of this century was the building of the spacious and handsome permanent hall, Jacobean in style by way of contrast to the early Tudor gothic of Blomfield's buildings. Its main adornment comes, however, from another source. For the excellent classical panelling at the high table end dates from the early years of the eighteenth century and was originally in the English church at Rotterdam. It was obtained by A. C. Benson, the Master of Magdalene, who had it set up in Selwyn in memory of his father, who had been Archbishop of Canterbury.

After the inevitable dislocation caused by the First World War, Selwyn settled down to complete the first half century of its career. Its undergraduate numbers, still kept down by the provision that all must live in college, were between 120 and 150 in the early 1930s, but had gone up to about 175 by the time the Second World War broke out. While one could not yet claim that any specially eminent position had been reached by any Selwyn man, much good and competent work was done in the college, and Selwyn's undergraduates included few, if any, of those who came up to Cambridge for little but social reasons. A new library by T. H. Lyon, who had remodelled the chapel at Sidney, was built as a war memorial and replaced a library installed in what had been the temporary chapel. By comparison with other colleges in Cambridge Selwyn was poorly endowed, but then, as in later years, it gained greatly from the prudent management of its resources.

Since 1945 Selwyn's history has largely been a process of closer assimilation to the normal pattern of a Cambridge college's life. Its higher than average proportion of men reading theology has given way to a more even balance between the subjects read in the college, with no particular preference for any one. The college now has about 330 undergraduate members, with some forty research and post-graduate students—a lower proportion than in most Cambridge colleges. Since 1957 Selwyn's Fellows, as in other colleges, have been the fully responsible governing body. The careful management of the college's affairs, always needed on account of Selwyn's modest endowments, continued after the war.

The Victorian buildings were much modernised, and some nearby houses were bought to provide more accommodation. Then, in the south-western corner of the court, the space between the hall and the entrance range was filled in with the new, compactly designed block which contains the senior and junior combination rooms; the architects are the well-known firm of Robert Matthew, Johnson-Marshall and Partners, who have designed the new University at Bath. More spectacular, and the biggest event in Selwyn's building history since the college came into being, is the great work of extension now completed across Grange Road. Selwyn found that its progress, under modern conditions where Cambridge colleges are, on an average, larger bodies than they were thirty years ago, was hampered by its shortage of buildings. An appeal was launched for money to pay for much-needed extensions. Most fortunately for Selwyn, this appeal attracted a most generous benefaction from the Cripps Trust, which has also provided the money for the newest buildings at St John's, which was Bishop Selwyn's college.

Selwyn College has thus been able, on a site bought from Jesus at the bottom of Cranmer Road, to build a complete new court, large enough to take 162 men, including some Fellows. Alone among Cambridge's many new buildings this court has been designed by the Nottingham architects Cartwright, Woollatt and Partners. Apart from its accommodation for Fellows, post-graduates and undergraduates, it has a post-graduates' parlour and a breakfast room. Selwyn can now offer accommodation in college to all of its post-graduates and undergraduates. It will thus return, on a basis of voluntary acceptance, to the position to which it was tied in its earliest days.

CHURCHILL

Of the three new colleges which now figure so largely in the townscape of north-western Cambridge, Fitzwilliam represents the revival, on a new site of an institution whose centenary, like that of Girton, fell in 1969. New Hall, again with a move from one site to another, is a mainly undergraduate college for women. The largest, and the most spread out of the three is Churchill, the one instance in post-war Cambridge of a wholly new college planned and built mainly for undergraduate members. It is, however, like Downing was in its earliest days, a college with a difference, so organised that a balance is kept, between its post-graduate and undergraduate members and between the subjects studied by Churchill members, which seems in tune with the needs of an increasingly technical age.

The idea that some new undergraduate college, with a slant towards science and technology, should be started in Cambridge was not wholly new by the middle of the 1950s, when Sir Winston Churchill gave up the premiership. It was soon after that political event that those who had such a foundation in mind linked their somewhat tentative project with the movement, originating with Sir Winston and his close entourage, which culminated in the actual foundation of Churchill College. Sir Winston, and his friend and adviser, Lord Cherwell, had for some time been worried at this country's low output, when compared with Soviet Russia and in relation to its population, of qualified technologists. The first project which they and others discussed was for some great technological college or University, to be located on its own and not necessarily in any town already containing a University.

But it appeared, among many arguments against such a scheme, that enormous sums would be needed to build and equip the laboratories and workshops which such an institution would obviously need, and that it would be better to place such a college in or near an existing University. An idea that some such college should be attached to the University of Birmingham was soon dropped. When in 1957 the project came up again, the Cambridge men who had already been thinking on somewhat similar lines were in part responsible for its revival, linking their own ideas for a new Cambridge college with the thought that such a college would attract support as a memorial to the life work of Sir Winston Churchill. If technology was to be the college's main subject the splendid laboratories of Cambridge, and its rich academic traditions and atmosphere, were at hand to help the new foundation on its way.

Industrialists who stand to benefit by employing the graduates of such a college were asked for their help; so, too, were various individuals and foundations in the United States. Consultations took place in Cambridge and early in 1958 the Senate approved the scheme for the new college It was to be named Churchill, its arms were to be a slightly altered version of those of the Churchills, and Sir Winston himself chaired the Trustees. Though not himself a University graduate he was Chancellor of the University of Bristol, and was keenly interested both in education in general and in this particular new venture. The final meeting at which the appeal details were settled was held in his London home.

The Trustees' appeal of 1958 asked for money to build and endow a large new college whose numbers would exceed those of all others in Cambridge but Trinity and St John's. It was to have some sixty Fellows, about 180 post-graduate students, and about 360 undergraduates; 500 undergraduates and post-graduates were to live in college.

A site off Madingley Road was chosen, and the Trustees held an architectural competition. The winner was Mr Richard Sheppard, of the London firm of Richard Sheppard, Robson and Partners. Mr Sheppard's plans, a good deal changed since their first acceptance, allowed for a set of central, or communal buildings, among them a large dining hall, an auditorium or assembly hall, a library, and a quiet reading room which would, like the college itself, be open all night. Important benefactors were responsible for three of these communal buildings in the new college. The Assembly Hall was the gift of the Isaac Wolfson Foundation. The Transport and General Workers' Union gave the Library, as a memorial to Churchill's wartime collaborator, Ernest Bevin, while the name of Lord Bracken, an old and close personal friend of Sir Winston, has been given to the impressive reading room fitted out in his memory.

For the first few years of its existence the status of Churchill was that of an

Approved Foundation. Its first Master, the eminent atomic scientist, Sir John Cockcroft, took up his post in 1959, and the first Fellows were elected in that same year.

Until the new college's Charter of Foundation was granted in the summer of 1960 its affairs remained in the hands of its Trustees. Early in that year work was started on the main buildings, and by the autumn of 1960 some of them were ready for use. An innovation in Cambridge was the provision, within the college and at the far end of the site from the main buildings, of some flats for married post-graduates. These flats, and a temporary dining hall, were the first of the college's buildings to be put up, but some of the flats were at first used to accommodate the college office which had started in a building in St Andrew's Street. As the appeal had met with a wide and generous response, and as more than £4,500,000 had come in by the early part of 1965 no trouble arose over the financing of the main building work. A few post-graduate students arrived at the beginning of the academic year of 1960–61, and Churchill's first undergraduates came up in the autumn of 1961.

The all-important buildings were now well under way. The hall and two residential blocks were finished early in 1964, and that important occasion, the first dinner in hall, was on March 26 of that year. On June 5 the college was formally opened by the Duke of Edinburgh who is its Visitor. By the end of that academic year the new college had fifty-two Fellows, one hundred and one post-graduate students, and 245 undergraduates; considerable increases, in all three categories, were achieved in the academic year which followed. Churchill was thus quick to deepen and consolidate its academic standing, and its rise to large numbers and to a varied social, sporting, and corporate life, was quicker than had been possible in Cambridge's older foundations.

The Assembly Hall, the Library, and the Bracken Reading Room were opened late in 1965, while the chapel at the far end of the site and close to the married post-graduate flats, was started early in the following year. No chapel had been included in the original scheme for the main college buildings, and some controversy arose over the idea that such a building would be appropriate in a college whose outlook was largely secular, and whose members included men of all beliefs and none. But there were many who felt that the college would be incomplete without some specifically religious building, and in the end the site of the chapel was leased by the Governing Body to those who were behind this particular venture. The Rev. Sir Timothy Beaumont came forward as the chapel's chief benefactor, while many gifts for fittings and furnishings came from other well-wishers. The chapel,

FITZWILLIAM. A general scene, South to North

CAVENDISH (now Homerton). The Hall and other buildings, looking East

SELWYN. The Chapel from the West, by Sir Arthur Blomfield

CHURCHILL. The main buildings; sculpture by Dame Barbara Hepworth

GIRTON. Gate Tower and Restless Gables, by Alfred Waterhouse

NEWNHAM. Clough Hall from the garden

attractively designed on a Greek cross plan, is now complete, and its use has not been hampered by its physical separation from the main complex of the college.

Though in the later months of 1968 work on some of the accommodation buildings in Churchill was still in progress most of them were by then complete. Except for a second, less expensive set of married graduates' flats by Mr David Roberts all the buildings have been put up to Mr Richard Sheppard's designs.

The general standard of planning and workmanship is very high, with the main construction of the buildings in an impressive blend of brick and concrete, and with much attractive flooring in polished yellow paving brick. Only the boiler chimney, high-rising and all too conspicuous as one approaches the college from Storey's Way, comes as a harsh and unsympathetic feature.

Unlike St Catherine's at Oxford, this great new Cambridge college has not been obliged to follow any rigid uniformity of design in its furnishings and embellishments. As in New Hall, its authorities have been free to go where they please for such items as chairs, crockery, knives, and forks. This flexibility has had very fortunate results with the college's wide range of gifts, presented in honour of its founder by European and Commonwealth countries, by various organisations and foundations, by many individual admirers of Sir Winston, and by members of the college. One thus sees a happy assortment of such things as the superb Lurçat tapestry from President de Gaulle, of timber for roofing and panelling from many Commonwealth countries, of Oscar Nemon's bust of the founder, and Dame Barbara Hepworth's outdoor sculpture, and of vigorous little wooden figures by various African artists. No feeling of incongruity arises in the face of such artistic diversity, and the way remains clear for varied future benefactions.

The year 1967 saw Churchill change from the status of an Approved Society to that of a college. Its post-graduates now numbered 150—not far below the target of 180 laid down for this element in the college's membership. Among these post-graduates are those who come over from the United States, with their stay in Cambridge financed by the United States Churchill Foundation. The money for this purpose was raised in the United States in memory of Sir Winston, and the American graduates who come over in this way work on Part II of various Cambridge Triposes, or else on research.

By the summer of 1968 the new college, with Prof R. W. Hawthorne as Master after the sad and sudden death of Sir John Cockcroft, had eighty

Fellows, its full complement of post-graduates and some 360 undergraduates. Science and technology were being studied by about seventy per cent. of the college's junior members. This proportion was a little more than that laid down in the Statutes, and it seems that some who might have come to Churchill with the idea of reading arts subjects are a little deterred, when they see the balance of subjects read in other and older colleges, by the heavily technological leaning of the great new college just north of Madingley Road. Yet the carefully balanced ideas of those who first thought of such a college in Cambridge, and who worked hard to set Churchill on its way were well fulfilled in the first decade of the new foundation's history.

Churchill has now, along with Clare and King's, become a pioneer among Cambridge Colleges in a move which would have seemed unthinkable only a few years ago. For it has admitted female undergraduates, with the same entry standards as for men and about equally distributed between those reading sciences and arts; there are also to be some woman graduate students. Thirty-two women came up to Churchill as undergraduates in the autumn of 1972, and a woman Fellow, already appointed, is to become a tutor. Churchill's female undergraduates are, for a start, to be housed in staircases reserved for them, but spread through the College so as to create mixed courts.

Another important development concerns the College's buildings. Adjoining the Bracken Library, by the same architects as the rest of the College, with a similar treatment of its concrete uprights, and with similar brickwork but with its windows relatively few and small, a new repository for the College's great collection of Churchill papers was well advanced by the beginning of 1973, and should be ready for its valuable contents by the end of the year.

GIRTON

THE founding of what eventually became Girton College was an important pioneering event in the wider movement towards the higher education of women. One dominant personality, along with many friends among those who were interested in her cause, was largely responsible for the commencement of the college.

The idea that women should share in some of the benefits of a Cambridge education tuned in with the general mid-Victorian move for University reform. An early development was in 1862, when a committee started to press for the admission of women to the Senior and Junior Cambridge Local Examinations. Their admission was actually approved in 1865. A leader in this new movement had been Miss Emily Davies, one of the two ladies who can be reckoned as the real foundresses of Girton.

Miss Davies was the daughter of an Anglican clergyman in the North. Among her friends was Elizabeth Garrett (later Elizabeth Garrett Anderson), whom she encouraged in her efforts to become Britain's first woman doctor. From about 1858, thanks to her friendship with another lady whose background was well in tune with 'progressive' ideas on the education and employment of women, she became active in the Women's Movement. Her collaborator was Miss Barbara Leigh Smith (later Mme Bodichon), the daughter of a Liberal Member of Parliament, a cousin of Florence Nightingale, and a close friend of the novelist George Eliot. Miss Smith had helped to found the 'Englishwoman's Journal', whose propaganda led to the starting of the Society for the Employment of Women. But if women were to be responsibly employed far more needed to be done for their education than what had so far been achieved by the efforts of governesses and Young Ladies' Academies.

Despite the success with the Cambridge Local Examinations Syndicate, Miss Davies soon felt that nothing but a residential college for women would meet the need. Mme Bodichon supported her, and in 1867 an appeal was launched. The committee sought help from such bodies as the associations for promoting women's higher education which now existed in the North, in Clifton, and elsewhere. George Eliot was an active supporter, the other woman novelist, Charlotte Yonge, was against the scheme, while the authoress Catherine Winkworth, though an active organiser of the Clifton Association for women's higher education, and despite a visit by Miss Davies to Clifton, found she could not approve of the project. Her brother, Stephen, was, however, an important benefactor of Newnham in its early days.

In 1868 the University started the Women's Local Examination, and planned special courses for those who wished to take it. These courses started in the next year, and Henry Sidgwick was the leading spirit behind their arrangement. The residential needs of the girls, who at first lived in lodgings, were to lead to the foundation of what in the end became Newnham College. But Miss Davies would have none of this particular scheme. Like Lilia in Tennyson's 'Princess', she would have the girls at her proposed college learn 'all that men are taught'. Their studies were to be the same as men's, and they were to sit, without any lowering of academic requirements, for the already recognised University examinations. Her college was, if possible, to be connected with the University, and its members were to have religious instruction according to Church of England principles. But on one vital point Miss Davies was adamant. Though Mme Bodichon hoped that the new college would be IN Cambridge, Emily Davies was sure that a fair distance was safer. Miss Davies's ideas prevailed, at first, over those of her friend. So, at what she felt to be the safe yet reasonably convenient distance of Hitchin, Benslow House was rented for the new venture, the Great Northern Railway being available to bring lecturers from Cambridge, but not to ferry the girls themselves to the fount of learning.

The little college opened, with only five students, in October, 1869. Some lecturers came from Cambridge by train, and the well-known theologian, F. J. A. Hort, then holding a living close to Hitchin, walked over from his rectory. Despite the small size of the community the formalities of academic life were duly observed, and the girls led a quiet, hardworking life. Numbers soon rose so that an iron building was put up in the garden to house students who there found that mice and nightingales were alike a nuisance.

In 1870 a party from Hitchin went to Cambridge to take 'Little Go'. But the small size of their buildings, and their isolation from good academic contacts, proved an increasing handicap, and as the lease at Hitchin was due to end in 1872 plans had to be made for a move. Miss Davies and some members of her committee were still against going to Cambridge or to any co-operation with the Cambridge Association for promoting women's higher education.

Their objections were largely social, and Miss Davies claimed that if such changes were made the ladies who supported her aims would be 'ashamed to speak' of the new college. Mme Bodichon, however, was all for Cambridge, and in the end there was a compromise. This was not achieved by halving the distance and settling at Royston but by choosing a site, 'near but not in' the University town, at the fork of the roads to Huntingdon and Girton village.

In 1872 the students at Hitchin numbered thirteen, and in the same year three of the girls gained Tripos successes, sitting their papers in a private room at the University Arms. Work was now progressing on the first block of Miss Davies's Castle Adamant at Girton, the architect being Alfred Waterhouse. A tutor and fifteen students took up residence in 1873. Then, and for many years afterwards, Miss Davies had little use for 'beauty and amenities' and would allow nothing to be spent outside her main purpose of furthering the education of women. So conditions at Girton were apt to be primitive and austere. Though the move to permanent buildings made new activities possible, and though the new college soon had a strong corporate life, things were in many ways difficult, the more so early because staff and student relations were not always of the best. Miss Davies was herself the Mistress of the College at the time of the move, but in 1875 a change came whereby the Mistress was to be outside the Governing Body but was the leader in the actual running of the college.

By 1884 Waterhouse's buildings could hold eighty students and some moves had been made, for Newnham students as well as those of Girton, towards a better status for women studying at Cambridge. Women could now take the Previous and Tripos examinations on the same conditions as the junior members of the University, and they could now make some use of the University Library. But in one important academic matter Girton girls differed from those of the other women's college now started in Cambridge. For while several Newnham students were up, for less than three years, with the Higher Local Examination as the ultimate goal, those at Girton took the same papers as men.

Soon after 1884 the college's first large legacy made it possible to build the Tower Wing, whose imposing main feature rises at the top end of the entrance avenue. It was by Paul Waterhouse, and the hue of its red brick and terracotta makes it look better in black and white photographs than in reality. The students soon numbered over one hundred, and were about 140 by 1895, when Directors of Studies were appointed. Miss Davies's target was two hundred, but this figure had not been reached by 1904, when her disagreement with various aspects of college policy caused her withdrawal from close involvement in the college's affairs. The main point of difference was over the strongly favoured idea that the teachers at Girton should have a much larger share in the college's government. Miss Davies was wholly against such a change and when her colleagues accepted the new idea she resigned her official posts at Girton, though continuing her interest in its welfare for the rest of a life of over ninety years.

Though the early years of this century saw a wider range of studies and college activities at Girton, and though numbers still slowly rose, finance was still a serious problem and a large fund-raising campaign was soon needed. But shortly before the first World War the generosity of Sir Alfred Yarrow, the well-known Clydeside shipbuilder, enabled the college to get free from debt. In 1919, which was the year of Girton's Jubilee, and when its students numbered about 180, the same benefactor came forward with endowments for research in physics, mathematics and science.

The 1920s were significant for two events. For in 1921 women up at Cambridge were allowed to take 'titular' degrees, and in 1924 Girton's Charter provided that the Mistress and Fellows were to be the Governing Body, with a College Council to run Girton's day-to-day affairs. By the early 1930s the buildings, as originally envisaged by Miss Davies, were completed, with Michael Waterhouse as the architect, and the user of more pleasingly tinted brick than that seen in the Victorian blocks.

Since 1945 Girton's history has been much conditioned by the admission of women as full members of the University. Since that event of 1948 its senior members have played an increasing part in the University's administration, they have sat on the Council of the Senate, and they have been on the Finance Board and other bodies.

Inside the college, great efforts have been made to keep up Girton's fine position in scientific studies. More than thirty per cent. of Girton's present-day undergraduates read science, there are several scientific Fellows, and four Girtonians are Fellows of the Royal Society. But a balance is maintained between science and the humanities. The college is popular for Arts subjects, and classics are still strong, as they were before the war. The college's Fellows are more numerous than they were, some of those now resident being married. Accommodation problems have been met in various ways. Graduate members, now some seventy in all, are some of them housed in graduate hostels, and they have had a parlour of their own for about twenty years, much longer than in many men's colleges. Girton's undergraduates now number about 370, nearly all living in college.

Though Girton's main buildings are still on the fringe of Cambridge the College is less isolated from the rest of the University than it was when Miss Davies reluctantly agreed to the move from Hitchin of her little band of students. The coming of Churchill, New Hall, and Fitzwilliam, and the general move of academic activity to sites west of the Backs, and in some cases to locations not far from Girton itself, have all combined to bring about a change. So too has the lunchtime use, by members of Girton, of the cafeteria now fitted out beneath the hall at Clare; as a result of these new facilities Girton has been able to close the rooms, in St Edward's Passage, which gave its members a central *piéd à terre*. More notable has been the building, by Girton itself, of its detatched court (known, from its chief contributor, as the Wolfson Court) on a site bought from St John's in Clarkson Road. The first part of this new court was occupied in October of 1971. It has a Fellow's flat and rooms for a hundred third-year undergraduates, with whom it has proved very popular. By David Roberts, with two long accommodation blocks flanking its central buildings, its inner parts display some of the most pleasing academic architecture in Cambridge. A pergola, and a narrow block with supervision rooms and a library, run parallel to each other, while a spacious entrance hall, a cafeteria and a dining room leading off it, and a very attractive Junior Combination Room surround a central patio whose effect of a Roman *impluvium* is increased by the Italianate pantiles of its inward-sloping roof.

NEWNHAM

HAD Emily Davies and Henry Sidgwick not disagreed over various educational and social matters, the women studying at Cambridge might at first have been concentrated not in two colleges but in one. The starting of what eventually became Newnham had its roots in the divisions between these two remarkable people, both on the right place for a women's college in the Cambridge area and on the course of studies its inmates were to pursue.

As the early history of Hitchin-Girton shows, Miss Davies insisted that the students who came to work under her should read the same subjects and take the same examinations as men. But in 1868 the University, largely at the instigation of the North of England Council for Promoting Women's Higher Education, also started the Women's Higher Local Examination. For this test some special courses of study were worked out. These were to a large extent organised by that pioneering figure Henry Sidgwick.

Late in 1869, a meeting to make detailed plans for women's lectures in Cambridge was held in the house of Professor Fawcett, the University's Professor of Political Economy. Lectures were started in the Lent Term of 1870. Girls who already lived in Cambridge could continue at home; a bigger problem was the housing of those who came from more distant places, the more so as some of them lived in what the mid-Victorians considered the horrifying conditions of unchaperoned lodgings.

The lodging problem of these earliest women students in Cambridge was solved, for a short time, by using the Regency house then known as 74 Regent Street, and now as the Glengarry Hotel. In the autumn of 1871 it was opened as a small house of residence. As at Hitchin two years earlier, the number of the students who lived there was only five. The Principal, Miss Anne Jemima Clough, had been the secretary of the North of England

NEW HALL. The Hall block, from along the Court

LUCY CAVENDISH. The College from the garden, summer 1972

DARWIN. A general view; late Georgian and Contemporary

Council. She proved an excellent choice as the first Principal of what in the end became Newnham College.

Next year, because her little group of students had increased, a move was made over the river, largely at the personal expense of Henry Sidgwick, to more spacious quarters in Merton Hall. The girls had lectures from some of Cambridge's best scholars. Sir John Seeley, the historian, who had journeyed to Hitchin to teach Miss Davies's girls, was among them. So too were Sidgwick, Jebb on the classics, Alfred Marshall, the famous economist, and Henry Jackson with his vast knowledge of ancient philosophy.

As the little society progressed Merton Hall also proved too small. Two adjacent houses in Bateman Street were taken until larger, permanent quarters were ready for use. The much-desired new buildings, on a site bought from St John's, were over the river at Newnham, a district less cut off from central Cambridge than Girton, but still relatively remote and still without Ridley Hall and Selwyn as neighbours for the women's college.

The Cambridge Association for Promoting Women's Lectures, formally set up in 1873, was the main organiser of the new scheme. It promoted a non-profit-making company which bought the site and built Old Hall, distinguished from the later buildings by Basil Champneys by the darker, more mellow red of its brickwork. It was opened in the autumn term of 1875 being occupied by Miss Clough and twenty-seven students. As the college, reflecting the spirit of Henry Sidgwick its real founder, was un-denominational and imposed no religious tests on its staff or on its would-be students, there was no chapel among the early buildings; nor has a chapel ever been built at Newnham.

Henry Sidgwick set the stamp of his personality and views on many aspects of the new college's early life. His approach to higher education was 'freer and more elastic' than that of Miss Davies. The girls reading pro-gramme was 'loose and empiric', and adapted to the needs and capacities of each student. Jane Harrison, later famous as a classical scholar and an authority on ancient Greek religion, was one of Newnham's earliest students. Most of those who entered the college went on to become teachers; Penelope Lawrence achieved prominence as the foundress of Roedean.

In 1879, when the Newnham Hall Company and the Lectures Association amalgamated, the new college had nearly eighty students, most of them living in a rented house outside the college. Advances had also been made, in the studies pursued, in the direction of what had always been the policy at Girton; and more Newnham girls were now reading for Cambridge's full honours course.

New buildings were clearly needed. Their provision led to an internal structure still unique in Cambridge. For another hall of residence was built, a little north of Newnham Hall, and parted from it by a public footpath. This was first called North Hall, the original building being South Hall. Clough Hall came next, and in 1891 the path between the first blocks was closed, the right of way being reinstated in the new road now known as Sidgwick Avenue.

Where these Halls of Newnham were remarkable was in the fair amount of independence, with their own dining halls and common rooms, which they possessed within the larger unity of the college. A Newnham student thus belongs to her Hall—Old, Sidgwick (as North Hall was renamed), Clough, or Peile, as well as being a member of the college.

At Newnham, the head of North Hall ranked as a Vice-Principal of the college. The first holder of the post was originally Miss Eleanor Mildred Balfour, Miss Clough's secretary; she was a sister of A. J. Balfour, the philosopher and future Prime Minister. In 1876 she married Henry Sidgwick and for three years the Sidgwicks lived in the new college—something of a phenomenon at a time when Cambridge was only just beginning (Masters' wives apart) to get accustomed to the mere notion of married dons.

By 1884, ninety women were up at Newnham. They could now sit for Tripos Honours, and some of them soon achieved great distinction. Two Newnhamites who were daughters of leading University reformers did particularly well. Mary Bateson, a daughter of the reforming Master of St John's, was outstanding as a historian, while in 1890 Philippa Fawcett, the daughter of Professor and Mrs Fawcett, was placed well above that year's senior wrangler.

By the end of last century, Newnham had securely attained the highest of academic standards. Its students now came from wider social circles, and included the winners of county and State Scholarships. A fourth Hall, named Peile Hall after the Master of Christ's and his wife who had, from the start, been the college's strong supporters was opened, in 1910, at the western end of the college. The gardens were a notable beauty of Cambridge; much of their charm was due to the care of Miss Blanche Athena Clough, Miss Clough's niece and biographer, who was Principal of Newnham for a short time after the First World War.

Newnham had more than two hundred students in 1914, and the war, with many Cambridge men enlisting and few freshmen coming up, soon had an unexpected effect on the college's numerical standing. In 1915 it ranked as the largest college in Cambridge; two years later its Royal Charter gave it full incorporation.

In the years between the wars, Newnham's numbers ran about even with those of Girton. In both colleges, academic standards were high; but Newnham's greater nearness to the town, and to the University's colleges, made it somewhat easier for Newnhamites to play their part in the societies and social activities of the University.

The Second World War, like the first, brought many changes to Newnham. For a time numbers actually went up, with a particular increase in those reading Natural Sciences, while problems of accommodation were increased, early in the war, by taking in some Bedford College staff, nurses, and other evacuees from London. By the end of the war, the courses of Girtonians and Newnhamites reading subjects other than science and medicine were shortened.

A great rush of new entrants followed the war, and Newnham had well over 350 women up in 1946. Subjects varied widely, and in 1949, the year after women attained full University membership, Mathematics, Natural Sciences, History, Modern Languages, English, Geography, and Classics were all well represented in the Newnham Tripos lists. Research graduates, as elsewhere in Cambridge, were more numerous than before the war.

When the Robbins Report came out, undergraduate numbers were put up by sixty, and more girls come from maintained schools than was once the case. Research graduates went up from sixty to about eighty, and Newnham's Fellows are also more numerous than before; some of them, as at Girton and New Hall, are married. There are now about 420 in residence, almost equally divided between the Arts and Science faculties. Natural Scientists, well up on their pre-war numbers, are the largest group. Social anthropology, including the study of developing countries, is also more popular.

Increased numbers naturally caused a demand for more accommodation. An appeal fund was launched, and more than £370,000, including a large donation from the Wolfson Trust, was raised by the end of 1967. Improvements in central heating were put in hand, also the wholly new block, on a Y-shaped plan, by Mr Christophe Grillet. This building, between the College's entrance off Sidgwick Avenue and the lane which runs up past the Principal's new Lodge, has been named the Strachey Building, after Miss Pernel Strachey (the author Lytton Strachey's sister) who was a recent Principal of Newnham; its residents are split between the existing halls. It is a useful, well planned addition to a College whose older buildings contrast sharply with the restrained colours and clean modernity of its lines. Its one defect—*experto crede*—is that on fine summer evenings one side of it is terribly hot.

NEW HALL

THE admission of women to the University in 1948 led to new thinking in Cambridge on the small number (two as against Oxford's five) of its women's colleges. While there were some who felt that the best policy would be to increase the endowments, and the numbers both of undergraduates and research workers, at Girton and Newnham, others considered that at least one new women's college was needed so that Cambridge could offer more places to women so as to balance its great, and continuing, preponderance of men. Discussions occurred in the early 1950s and the first action was soon taken to fulfil the second of the two debated policies; the University itself had now agreed to an increase in its female undergraduates provided a new and autonomous college came into being for their housing and to act as their social centre.

New Hall, like Newnham, owed some of its beginning to a meeting in a drawing room. This time, in 1952, the venue was not the Fawcetts' house in Brookside, but in the Grecian setting of the Master's Lodge in Downing. Lady Whitby was the hostess, and among the ladies present were Mrs Parsons, Miss Ena Mitchell and Mrs White, the Bursar of Newnham. This meeting led to the starting of what was first called the Third Foundation Association. Dame Myra Curtis, then the Principal of Newnham, was its chairman, and Mrs G Burkill was also very active in the movement. Only with the detailed planning of the new foundation, with its echo of Oxford and of William of Wykeham in its name of New Hall, did the name of the association change to that of the New Hall Association.

Things moved swiftly after the meeting in Downing, and as the foundation process of New Hall is a recent matter it is easy to track. It was the first of the colleges now existing in the University to be founded so close to the present time that many who played a part in its beginnings, and who were eye witnesses and participants in what occurred, are still active in Cambridge.

The New Hall Association, soon becoming a limited company, rented a house, at the far end of Silver Street and close by the junction of Queen's Road and Sidgwick Avenue, which is now part of Darwin College and which lies close to the Newnham Grange territory so delectably enshrined by Mrs Gwen Raverat in 'Period Piece'. In 1954 the Hall opened, like the little societies at Hitchin and in 74 Regent Street on a very small scale though a little more substantially than did those embryos of Girton and Newnham. Miss A. R. Murray, entitled the Tutor, had one Fellow as a colleague, and there were sixteen undergraduates. The initial status of the new foundation was somewhat dauntingly expressed as a 'Recognised Institution for Women'. New, spacious, and permanent buildings were in mind from the start; the main problem was the raising of the necessary money.

Funds soon started to come in, and of the older colleges St John's and King's were specially generous. Some money came from the Colston Educational Trust, some from the Nuffield Foundation, and some from the Soroptimists and from various girls' schools. The University gave a sum, made over to it by the Government through the University Grants Committee, which had first been set aside for the scientific buildings projected for the area near the Cavendish Laboratory. The 'Orchard' estate, on the Huntingdon Road and next to the transferred Fitzwilliam House, was chosen for the new college. Half of it was given by the University and half by the two sisters, Mrs Rees Thomas and Lady Barlow, the daughters of Horace Darwin and thus cousins of Mrs Raverat. Chamberlin, Powell, and Bon were chosen as the college's architects, and the initial scheme allowed for two hundred members, 170 of these being undergraduates. But it was not until 1962 that work started on the present buildings of New Hall. In the meantime, the college's growing social life was centred on Silver Street, being carried on under considerable difficulties.

Entrance to New Hall in its early days was mainly by interview, but also with one examination, and between 1954 and 1960 some 150 undergraduates came up to the college; of these an eighth were from overseas. In 1961, the new college had eight senior members, thirteen research graduates, and the respectable number of sixty-six undergraduates. Its academic achievements, like those of the two other women's colleges were high, and New Hall could actually claim that its members scored a higher percentage of firsts than the Tripos examinees of any other college in Cambridge. Social and collegiate life was still centred in the Silver Street house, but five others had been rented to provide more sleeping accommodation.

By 1964 more than £1,100,000 had been raised for New Hall, and in the academic year of 1964–65 the first members moved into the first completed part of their new residential buildings. A few Fellows and six undergraduates formed the initial party, sleeping in their own buildings but taking meals in the neighbouring, and hospitable colleges of Fitzwilliam and Churchill. New Hall's undergraduates, with a wide range of studies, by then numbered over a hundred.

From 1965 onwards, the transfer to the new buildings proceeded gradually as work was completed. At the start of the academic year 1965–66 half of New Hall's members were on the Huntingdon Road site. The Silver Street buildings were kept on until the end of 1965, but for the academic year of 1966–67 all New Hall's members were brought together in the living and social quarters provided by the new blocks.

All of the rooms so far built are now occupied, and New Hall has some thirty-five research graduates and about 280 undergraduates; nearly all of the last named are resident in college. The ultimate target, when the neighbouring site of 'The Grove' is available for expansion, and when the architects' plans have all been carried out, is about three hundred junior members.

Chamberlin, Powell, and Bon's buildings for New Hall are among the most striking academic groupings in Cambridge. Though concrete enters largely into their construction, bricks of an unusual whiteness, specially made in Tunbridge Wells, have also been used. The three-tiered library, with its barrel vault, is a specially fine building, while the Junior Combination Room projects from the hall block into the enclosed space of the college's inner court. The hall is the most novel, and in some ways the most controversial, of the college's new buildings. Unlike all other college halls in Cambridge its plan is that of a Greek cross, with the high table placed to one side of the dining space and not in the middle as was first suggested, in one of the cross's equal limbs. The hall, like the similarly planned library, which the same architects designed for the Grammar School at Cheltenham, is surmounted by a dome.

Further building plans have yet to be decided in detail, but it will certainly be necessary to increase the amount of living accommodation available for undergraduates, while a lodge for the President is another desirable addition. Furniture, carpets, and other gifts are not necessarily an integral part of the architect's overall plan; in this respect New Hall differs from Arne Jacobsen's tautly integrated buildings for St Catherine's College at Oxford.

By now, New Hall has existed long enough for its past *alumnae* to number well over seven hundred. One of its graduates, having held a Fellowship, is now teaching overseas, another is a resident Fellow, while a third is a research Fellow. Two women who came to New Hall on post-graduate research now hold University research posts at Cambridge, while several New Hall graduates are in teaching posts in other Universities. Though the fledgling college's corporate life was strong under the difficult residentially dispersed conditions of its early life is no less strong in New Hall's quarters off Huntingdon Road; experience has shown that girls who have already been resident in college are reluctant to move out into hostel accommodation in other houses.

A further stage has now been reached in New Hall's attainment of full collegiate status. A Royal Charter has been granted, and under its terms, in July of 1972, New Hall officially became a College of the University with its own Statutes and an endowed income. Of the money raised to put up the buildings very little could be set aside for the College's endowment. But an endowed income, ever since the thirteenth-century first days of Merton and Peterhouse, has been of the essence of an 'Oxbridge' College. Some other Cambridge Colleges have now put up substantial sums for the future endowment of New Hall.

LUCY CAVENDISH

Of the new graduate foundations which have since 1962 come into being in Cambridge, Darwin and Wolfson Colleges and Clare Hall exist, in the main, to provide social and collegiate facilities for senior or more junior post-graduates, both men and women, who are pursuing an uninterrupted academic life. Nearly all of the Fellows in these colleges are male and they also form a majority of their post-graduate students. Lucy Cavendish College, only a little junior to Darwin and Wolfson, got the status of an Approved Society in the summer of 1965. It started as a graduate college for women only, and like the other graduate colleges it gave a social gathering place to its members, these being women who, though they hold teaching posts in the University or are engaged in various post-graduate studies, do not belong to the three older women's colleges in Cambridge. More important, for many of its members and in the opinion of those who worked to found the society, is the chance which it offers to academically qualified women, whose University career has been temporarily broken by work or family ties, to come back into the full stream of academic life. Its physical facilities were at first modest. Now, with the taking over of more spacious quarters, the college's opportunities are much increased.

Like some other institutions, Lucy Cavendish College originated in talks over meals; the origins of the University itself may not have been very different. Discussions were held in 1951, over several weekly lunches in the Regent House members' combination room which had recently been opened in the Old Senate House. Those discussions led to the creation of a women's graduate college. Those who held them were Dr Anna Bidder, Mrs Margaret Braithwaite and Dr Kathleen Wood-Legh. Those pioneers realised that there were some women in Cambridge, with high academic qualifications and engaged on teaching work, who belonged to the Regent House, but who were not Fellows of Colleges. They felt that, for such women, some organised society would meet a real need, even though it might start without its own premises. Such a society was therefore formed. The occasions of cohesion for its *commensales* took the form of regular dinners, at first in the Copper Kettle restaurant but eventually, through the kindness of the Master and Fellows, in the Harvey Court of Caius. This dining group continued for fourteen years, providing valuable social contacts for its members who put up what were described, in a Senate report of 1965, as 'fruitful ideas' on ways in which the Cambridge collegiate system might be adapted to meet changed conditions. A report on this subject was sent to the Bridges Syndicate during its meetings of 1961 and 1962.

The dining group also gave some help to women who were not members of the Regent House, but who were taking part in University teaching, usually as supervisors. By 1965, in which year this informal but definite group applied to the University for recognition as an Approved Society, and when the Council of the Senate reported on its future, some fifty women had belonged to it; about twenty to thirty were at that time its active members.

The council, noting the 'national importance' of the poor use made of the talents of professional women whose careers had been interrupted, agreed that such a society could give these women a chance to retrain themselves by advanced study or by getting higher qualifications. Its first concern would be with fairly senior graduates, but some of those with more recent degrees could also be admitted. The council recommended the society's recognition; it had already decided to obtain for it, from Magdalene College, a ten-year lease of two attractive little eighteenth-century houses in Northampton Street which soon succeeded two small offices in Silver Street as the new society's headquarters.

On July 31, 1965, the University gave its recognition to the new society; its legal establishment, with Dr Bidder as its first president, came two months later. The name of Lucy Cavendish was now, at the suggestion of some of its members, given to the society, thus honouring an aristocratic lady, somewhat comparable, in her own time, to Lady Clare and Lady Pembroke in the fourteenth century, who had married into a great family which did much for Cambridge and who herself had a deep interest in the education of girls and young women. Lady Lucy Cavendish, a sister of a well-known headmaster of Eton and of the first Master of Selwyn, and a niece of Mr Gladstone, was the widow of Lord Frederick Cavendish, the Chief Secretary for Ireland who, in 1882, was murdered in the Phoenix

Park at Dublin. She was thus a daughter-in-law of the seventh Duke of Devonshire who was a most active and zealous Chancellor of the University of Cambridge. Lady Lucy was childless and never remarried, devoting the rest of her long life to religious, charitable, and educational causes. She took much interest in St Mary's College, Paddington, and in the Girls' Public Day School Trust. Her membership of the Royal Commission on Secondary Education, and her work for women's education in Yorkshire, led to an Honorary Degree from the University of Leeds, the first given by that University to a woman. Not herself a graduate, she was suggested, in 1885, as a suitable person to fill the vacant post of Mistress of Girton.

From 1965 onwards, Lucy Cavendish College was better able to pursue its aim of giving social facilities in Cambridge to women whom its founders specially wished to help, and more post-graduate research workers could now be added to its numbers. Though they were small and cramped, the two cottages in Northampton Street provided basic office space and a small common room where tea, coffee and light meals could be provided. Since 1967 the society's dinners have been held in Churchill College. Numbers steadily rose, so that there are now about 120 women on the Lucy Cavendish books. Thirty-two of these are Fellows, and a few are Research Fellows. Some two dozen, in Cambridge on teaching, academic writing, and research, rank as senior members, while others are post-graduate students researching for doctorates or for other purposes. A few others, on various studies or writing work, are in the newest category of 'members'.

A new phase in the history of Lucy Cavendish started with the College's move, in 1970, to a building far more spacious than the two houses which were its previous headquarters, and which are still kept to provide much needed accommodation. St John's has leased the new College a large late Victorian house, in Lady Margaret Road whose name is that of another of Cambridge's great widowed benefactresses. Till recent years the house was used by the Anglican Franciscans who are now in Botolph Lane. Earlier still, it was the mother house of the Oratory of the Good Shepherd where Fr Wilfred Knox presided, and where Mr Malcolm Muggeridge could often, in his earlier days, be encountered in seeking conversation. Redecorated, and with what was once the chapel now used as a library and quiet room, its new home gives Lucy Cavendish more office space and better social facilities, while some students' rooms have been fitted out on the top floor. A scheme for extra buildings, starting with a dining hall which can be used for various purposes, has been prepared by Mr John Meunier and Mr Barry Gasson of the University School of Architecture; the building has been designed with a blank wall on one side so as, in some measure, to exclude the inhumane cacophony of the heavy commercial traffic which now grinds its way up and down Lady Margaret Road. Planning permission has been granted for the hall's erection when funds allow.

There is also the institutional change, approved in 1972, whereby Lucy Cavendish College is now allowed to take undergraduates. Some of these are to be 'mature' students, aged 25 and upwards and in some cases married. The college's total undergraduate strength is not to exceed fifty, and Lucy Cavendish's first undergraduates, 22 in number, came up in 1972. As they are not of the age usual for most Cambridge undergraduates there is a considerable unification of age groups, in this newest of the women's colleges, between the younger Fellows, those reading for the degree of Bachelor of Education, and the undergraduates who have recently arrived.

DARWIN

THOUGH nearly all of Cambridge's ancient colleges started their careers as havens of endowed security and regular living for senior members of the University, none of them continued, as All Souls' at Oxford has done, as purely post-graduate foundations. Only since the Second World War has Cambridge seen the growth of post-graduate colleges, conceived, in large measure, to meet the social needs of those who have come from many other Universities and, indeed, from many countries, to avail themselves of Cambridge's fine facilities for research.

The first of these foundations to get formally established was Darwin College, now well into its career, at the far end of Silver Street and close by that street's junction with Queen's Road and Sidgwick Avenue, on its commanding, somewhat noisy but very attractive site. Research students from other Universities started to come to Cambridge as far back as 1896 and their numbers greatly increased after the Ph.D. degree had been instituted in 1920. In the last year before the war Cambridge had more than four hundred of these graduate students. Some years earlier, in 1932, Professor Sir Ernest Barker and some friends had submitted to the Council of the Senate a memorandum urging the foundation of a graduate college whose main emphasis would be on research. It seems, however, that this prescient project was not considered, and war came before any action could be taken to found some sort of a Cambridge equivalent to All Souls'.

In the last year of the war, Dr Hele, the Master of Emmanuel who was then Vice-Chancellor, publicly recommended a graduate college, linking his proposal to the (since unrealised) idea that the undergraduate colleges should not allow more than ten per cent. of their membership to consist of post-graduate students. No action was taken on this particular suggestion, but the idea was kept alive and in the years after 1947 the notion was often ventilated.

A specially energetic advocate of the idea was Mr M. McCrum, Senior Tutor of Corpus and a leading figure behind his own college's development of the Leckhampton site to house some of its own post-graduates. An important influence which made for the acceptance of a graduate college in Cambridge was the report of the syndicate, under the chairmanship of Lord Bridges, which had been set up to consider the relationship between the University and the colleges; this had started work in 1960 and reported in 1962. The syndicate took the view that a graduate college ought to come into being, and that it would be a 'new and valuable element in the University.' Its members were helped towards this view by a memorandum, put in by Mr McCrum and Professor F. G. Young, which stressed the way in which such a college could help visiting scholars to get integrated into Cambridge's collegiate life.

When the Bridges Report was out, the foundation process of Cambridge's first graduate college went ahead reasonably fast. The main initiative, and the chief financial support, for the new venture came from the three existing colleges of Caius, St John's and Trinity. Discussions went on during 1962 and early in 1963, and in June of 1963 the intention of the three colleges to found the new one was formally made known. By that time, moreover, it was possible to announce both the name of the new foundation and a large part of its eventual site.

Sir Charles Darwin, once the Master of Christ's and more recently the Director of the National Physical Laboratory, had died on the last day of 1962. He was a son of Sir George Darwin. He had made his home at his father's old house, Newnham Grange, which had by the time of his death been delightfully enshrined in the pages of his sister Mrs Gwen Raverat's 'Period Piece'. Sir Charles' death, and the move from Cambridge of the remaining members of his family, made Newnham Grange and the Old Granary available for other purposes. Lady Darwin and her relatives favoured the idea that the house and its waterside grounds should accommodate a college whose spatial needs would clearly be less than those of the old foundations with their many undergraduate members. They also agreed that the name of the new graduate college should perpetuate that of the Darwins.

Much of the preliminary work had thus been done by the time that the scheme to found Darwin was publicly launched. The new college's trustees were formally set up in the summer of 1964, and they soon decided to found it 'for the advancement in education, learning and research'. In 1965 Darwin

College won recognition as an 'Approved Foundation' and was thus placed almost on the same official level as the colleges whose funds do not have to be administered by trustees.

The new college's members, at first to number about eighty, were to be a mixture of Fellows (most of them in University teaching posts) and of post-graduate research workers. The range of the college's subjects was to be wide and comprehensive, covering both the arts and various scientific disciplines. Professor Young was appointed the first Master of Darwin, and the college's principal officers, along with some of its Fellows, were soon named.

Then, in the summer of 1964, news came of the great benefaction which enabled the new college to plan for its really important expansion. The man who so notably came to Darwin's aid was Mr Max Rayne, acting in large measure through the Max Rayne Foundation, whose trustees are still giving ten annual instalments, each of them of £50,000, for the 'general benefit' of the new college. So important, for Darwin's early days and for its future, are these gifts that the arms of Rayne impale those of Darwin to form the college's coat. The most apparent result of the Rayne benefaction has been the physical expansion of Darwin's buildings, and the way in which Newnham Grange is linked to another house, a little later than itself, which has its place both in 'Period Piece' and in post-war Cambridge's academic history.

Though Darwin's numbers make it unnecessary to allow for really large buildings, more room was soon seen to be needed than that provided by the Newnham Grange property. The large next-door house, known as The Hermitage, and in the late Victorian days of Gwen Raverat's childhood the home of the rich old lady with eight servants, a little black dog, and a carriage and pair, had in 1954 been the initial home of New Hall. But at the time of Darwin's foundation New Hall was soon due to move to its new quarters on the Huntingdon Road. Darwin's founders thus reckoned that the Hermitage and its garden would soon be available for their purposes, the more so as St John's, one of their founding colleges, owned the house. When, at the end of 1965, Miss Murray and her colleagues left the building, the Darwin Trustees soon bought the property. Everything between the Old Granary and the northern end of Newnham Terrace was thus available for the conversion work and new construction which had already been planned, and which has now been very successfully finished.

Messrs Howell, Killick, Partridge and Amis were appointed as Darwin College's architects. What they achieved, with remarkable skill, is the conversion to the college uses of the existing buildings, the connection of

Newnham Grange and The Hermitage by a new block (of three storeys and not, as in the older houses, of two) and at the far end of the site the building of a remarkably fine and impressive octagonal hall which almost touches one end of Newnham Terrace. This hall has been raised up to first-floor level and from its windows, or from the balcony at the top of its stairway to the garden, a good enfilading view along the backs of all the college's buildings shows that Darwin can boast waterside 'backs' as charming as any in Cambridge.

The linking block between The Hermitage and Newnham Grange has been most carefully and sensitively designed and is excellent in nearly all its details. Large kitchens have been fitted out in The Hermitage, while one room in Newnham Grange has been furnished as a late Victorian period piece, with Morris wallpaper and other appropriate details.

Loans from the Darwin family include a Regency-type book-case which once stood in Charles Darwin's home at Downe, while among various family portraits one, by Wright of Derby, is of the naturalist's grandfather Erasmus Darwin; it is a nice irony that the site of the house wherein it hangs could have been seen, from Queens' across the river, by the most famous bearer of the Erasmus name.

Darwin's Fellows and post-graduates started to arrive late in 1965, a few months before the Newnham Grange part of the site was first occupied. By the Michaelmas term of 1966 the Fellows numbered twenty-one, and there were forty-six post-graduate students. From 1966 onwards women were admitted, amounting to about thirty per cent. of the whole.

Rather more than half of the 248 graduate members of Darwin are working on scientific subjects. Most of the Fellows are in University teaching posts, while eleven per cent. of the post-graduates have come from other Cambridge colleges. Other British Universities have members at Darwin, while more than forty per cent. of the college's present post-graduates have come from overseas. This is a lower proportion than a few years back, but the forty countries now represented give a wider geographical range than ever before. Nearly forty of these overseas students are from Commonwealth countries, while 16 are from the United States. Others, from Europe, Asia, African states, and Latin America make Darwin a truly international community. The figures, and the details of the subjects in which Darwin men and women are researching, certainly suggest that the college is fulfilling the purpose which its Master (now knighted) long had in mind.

WOLFSON

originally

(UNIVERSITY COLLEGE)

In the section on the origins and history of Darwin College I explained that a powerful influence which made for its successful launching was the issue, in 1962, of the Bridges Report on the relationship between the University and the colleges. Though the members of the Bridges syndicate felt that the creation in Cambridge of a graduate centre should come before the foundation of a purely graduate college they also made the point that they would like to see the creation of such a college.

What actually happened, by the very middle of 1965, was the foundation in Cambridge not of one graduate college but of two. I have dealt with the foundation, by three ancient and historic colleges, of Darwin College. The other initiative, in our own century compensating for a failure over six centuries back, came from the University itself.

The idea that the University should maintain an endowed establishment for the teaching of theology and other subjects went back as far as 1321, when the then chancellor got a royal licence to amass modest funds for this purpose. Nothing came of this particular scheme, but it was to some extent fulfilled when in 1326 Richard de Badew founded the small graduate society of University Hall. He himself, with help from the then Bishop of Norwich, found the money for the scheme, but the houses in which these early scholars lived were University property.

But the University did very little to support the new foundation, so that when de Badew met with financial trouble he had to turn for aid to Lady Clare who duly, with the University's consent, took over the whole foundation and gave it her name.

Such was the somewhat pathetic end of what might have been the

ST EDMUND'S HOUSE. The Long Frontage, looking towards the Chapel

WOLFSON. A view from the garden, summer 1972

CLARE HALL. Residential Buildings and 'Family Walk'

HUGHES HALL. The Main Buildings, a general view

medieval University's own venture in college sponsorship. It has been left to our own age, and to a much transformed University, to see that University founding a college on its own.

The Bridges Syndicate having reported in 1962, the discussions which led the University to found its graduate college must have been going on at the same time as those which culminated in the foundation of Darwin. As it happened, the date of Darwin's foundation came five months earlier in 1965 than the formal inauguration of University College whose trust deed, making it separate from the University which had founded it, was signed on June 30 of that year. The University's practical aid came with its gift of the college's site and with financial help, after two initial years, at the rate of £20,000 a year for a total of ten years in all.

The site itself comprises Bredon House, built some sixty years ago at the far end of Selwyn Gardens and the home, before its purchase by the University and some temporary use by New Hall, of Professor Gardiner who held the chair of botany. Very appropriately, in view of the identity and tastes of its last private owner, the house has a large, very beautiful garden which stretches down as far as Barton Road.

University College started in a very small way, with some half-dozen post-graduate students in the academic year of 1966-7. Its more significant beginning was in October of 1967, with thirty-five junior members in that year and an increasing number of Fellows. The Council of the Senate hoped that the new college's Fellows would, within its first three years, reach a total of sixty. The rate of expansion was in fact much quicker, for University College had sixty-six Fellows in the summer of 1968, with thirteen visiting Fellows from various other Universities, most of them from overseas. As in Darwin, many of the Fellows hold University teaching or administrative posts. The college's post-graduate students are about 200 in the academic year 1972-73.

Not many of these members can so far live in college, and the physical expansion of the College is only now seriously under way. Bredon House, with a temporary extension running out into the garden and containing the hall, remains the college's social and office headquarters.

But four nearby houses, two of them so close as to count as being 'in college', have been bought to house some of the post-graduates. One building, in 'temporary-permanent' construction, has also been added to one side of Bredon House. Moreover, a project has now been started whereby suitable parts of the College's site will be filled with buildings of a more obviously collegiate type. Messrs Ferrey and Mennim, York architects with no previous University experience, have got out a scheme, replacing one which they prepared some four years ago, for buildings which will leave Bredon House, most of the garden, and the avenue of trees running up from the Barton Road, intact, but which will provide important buildings for University College's corporate and residential life. The most notable single block will be square, at the bottom of the garden, and will contain a hall to seat about a hundred diners, combination rooms, and squash courts. The avenue, in a way recalling the one at Trinity, will still bisect the property, and most of the residential blocks, of three or four storeys and each containing five staircases, will be faced with brownish yellow brick and will lie West of the avenue. Some of them will be grouped, in the traditional Cambridge manner, round a small court. It is on these blocks that considerable progress had been made by the beginning of 1973. Their completion, along with that of the main part of the building scheme, is now assured by a great benefaction which has clarified the future of the college and has also changed its name.

During 1972 the college authorities asked the Wolfson Foundation if it could make a large grant which would help their college both with its building project and with the financing of its varied activities. Should this be found possible the renaming of University College could fitly recognise both this particular act of generosity and the many benefactions which Sir Isaac Wolfson and his associates have made to Cambridge. A grant of £2,000,000, to be spread over five years, was duly arranged, and University College became Wolfson College on 1 January 1973. As the 'University Reporter' put it, these events have been 'interestingly reminiscent' of the transformation, over 600 years ago, of University Hall into Clare College. Sir Isaac has also become the first eponym since the Trinity, its second Person, St Mary Magdalene, St Catherine to give his name to a college at both Oxford and Cambridge.

One idea for the detailed use of the new buildings is that one block should be set aside for those who come to University College from Continental countries. Those visitors form but one of the college's wide-ranging contacts with the world outside Cambridge. The years since the war have, of course, seen a great increase, throughout the University, in these links. They are, however, fostered to a special extent in Wolfson College. Many of its visiting Fellows come from Continental Universities, while research Fellowships in European studies are also being established. Visiting Fellows are also to come from Universities in underdeveloped countries, whether in the Commonwealth or elsewhere. These overseas connections go along with projects whereby Wolfson College has become the link point between the University and some sections of this country's business and administrative life which have not, so far, had particularly strong connections with academic circles.

One such activity provides for a term's residence for non-graduate junior managers in commerce and industry. Such a course was, for some twenty years, run in Cambridge by the Y.M.C.A.; this has now been centred in Wolfson College. These young managers attend lectures and supervisions, widening their knowledge and outlook in the subjects of their choice, and gaining a first-hand knowledge of University life not always possessed by those whose training for their work has been mainly technical or vocational. Banks, and firms like I.C.I. and Cadbury's have already successfully sent junior members on this course.

This idea of a short spell at Cambridge for those who work elsewhere may also be extended so as to make a Cambridge term possible for administrative officers of the Greater London Council, and perhaps for some from other important local authorities.

Less of an innovation, but designed to make Wolfson College the home of a training scheme long established in Cambridge, is the plan whereby the 'Overseas Administrative' course is concentrated there. Earlier on, it gave Colonial Service officers a spell of specialised study before taking up their overseas appointments. They were formerly dispersed among various colleges; in future they will all, under their present title, come to Wolfson College.

Another project, more obviously and closely linked to the academic life of Cambridge itself, has made Wolfson the chief base for some detailed research into sixth-form curricula and into the relationship between work done in schools and the studies pursued at Oxford and Cambridge.

Sir Desmond Lee, the well-known Corpus Christi man who has been headmaster both of Clifton and Winchester, was made a Senior Research Fellow and is the director of the inquiry, his assistant director being at work at the Oxford end. Research of this kind, and its application, could lead to a better continuity between work done in school and what undergraduates read when they come up to Cambridge. The choice of University College as the Cambridge centre of such an inquiry arose from the wide range and experience of the college's senior members.

Other new projects concern nutrition, and conservation and various subjects connected with it. Research Fellows, expert in different aspects of these wide-embracing topics, will get facilities to meet, and to work together, in the College, which will thus become the co-ordinating factor in what should be some fruitful interdisciplinary studies. These most recent schemes show how various and flexible are the ways in which this particular post-graduate foundation can help Cambridge itself and the world outside it.

ST EDMUND'S HOUSE

MOST of the post-graduate colleges which have lately started in Cambridge have been wholly new foundations, though some of their buildings, as at Darwin, have long stood within their sites. One of them, however, has won through, to the status of an approved society within the University, from a previous existence which goes back to the last decade of the nineteenth century. Its buildings, moreover, are in part those built for another academic institution which did not last long enough to occupy them.

On its agreeable sloping site off Mount Pleasant, St Edmund's House, not in its name commemorating the martyred East Anglian king, but for special reasons keeping green in Cambridge the name of the patron saint of Oxford's St Edmund Hall, has had an interesting, at one time controversial past. It also seems set, with the prospect of new buildings put up to hold larger numbers, to have a future career of widely varied use.

Though a few Roman Catholics had come up to Cambridge in the nineteenth century, their residence was, for most of that period, very much discouraged. But after Cardinal Manning's death, and under the relatively relaxed régime of Leo XIII, the situation eased a little. From 1895 onwards, and after Cardinal Vaughan had given his somewhat reluctant consent, the residence of Catholic laymen at the two ancient Universities was 'tolerated' by their ecclesiastical superiors. An Oxford and Cambridge Catholic Board was specially set up to arrange lectures which would protect them from 'false and erroneous teaching'. The leading Cambridge member, resident in Cambridge and making his home a social centre for the few undergraduates of his faith, was Baron Anatole von Hügel.

The idea soon grew up, among some of England's leading Catholic laity, that the academic benefits of a University education might be made available to most of those in England who were studying for the Roman Catholic priesthood. The link with Cambridge was established through St Edmund's College, whose extensive buildings stand, a few miles north of Ware, just off the main London to Cambridge road.

This college had been established in Hertfordshire to carry on part of the work done, in penal times when the training of priests was impossible in England, of the English College at Douai in Flanders. The College of St Edmund's, like that at Ushaw near Durham, stands in direct continuity with the Douai College started in 1568. It had long been associated with London University, and in 1896 it became an affiliated college of Cambridge. A move was then made to start an offshoot in Cambridge itself, bearing the same name as the parent college and making it possible for students to keep six of the nine terms needed for graduation. Fr Edmond Nolan, who later became Master of St Edmund's House, came in charge of the little colony, living in the presbytery of Our Lady and the English Martyrs church in Hills Road but also instructed to find buildings in which St Edmund's, at first consisting of two laymen and two church students, could in time expand. Largely thanks to the generosity of the then Duke of Norfolk, the nucleus of the present buildings on Mount Pleasant solved the immediate problem.

The block bought for St Edmund's House had been started, but never used, by the recently defunct Ayerst Hostel; a short digression on its story will not, in this record of Cambridge collegiate history, be out of place.

It had been started in 1884 by the Rev. William Ayerst, a Caius man and a staunch Evangelical. Like his father, whose missionary yearnings had been directed by Charles Simeon, he was especially keen on the Christianising of Jews. He was once principal of the Hebrew Missionary College, and like his father served at the Jews' Episcopal Chapel in London. It seems, from the presence on the staff of Ayerst Hostel of a Hebrew lecturer, that some of the ordinands who were to reside there were expected to take up this particular work. In other respects, and particularly in the way in which it made residence at Cambridge possible for men of small means, Ayerst's foundation resembled Cavendish College. It commenced in some houses in Queen Anne Terrace along Gonville Place.

But although Ayerst spent much of his own money on the property conditions there were far from ideal: entrance at night was difficult to arrange, and the proctors were dissatisfied with the discipline kept in the hostel. Completely new buildings seemed to be the solution, so that late in 1893 Mr Ayerst got the University's licence to open as a hostel some new houses in Mount Pleasant. In two years' time he was permitted to open his 'lately erected' buildings. But serious, largely financial, difficulties soon arose. During 1896 the work of Ayerst Hostel came to an end, and by the end of that year the Non-Collegiate Students' Board was empowered to admit Ayerst's members.

The Catholic successors to Mr Ayerst in the ownership of the simple, undistinguished Mount Pleasant buildings occupied them during 1896. Two serious disadvantages soon appeared. One was that the foundation had been made without finding out if the Roman Catholic bishops of England and Wales would in fact send any students there. Secondly, it proved impossible for St Edmund's House, though soon incorporated under the Companies Act, to get University recognition as a Public Hostel.

The attempt, in the spring of 1898, to gain that recognition led to one of the great controversies of late Victorian Cambridge. Ingrained anti-Catholic feeling, stronger among non-resident Cambridge graduates than those on the spot, was mixed with genuine doubts as to whether such a foundation as St Edmund's would fit into the University as a whole. Dr Armitage Robinson, later Dean of Wells, was a prominent advocate of the recognition of St Edmund's; as a Christ's man he may, in later years, have helped, as he certainly did with the Benedictine student monks from Downside, in establishing his own college's hospitable link with the students at St Edmund's.

Other leading Cambridge men (several of them agnostics) who supported the house's recognition were Oscar Browning, Montagu Butler the Master of Trinity, Henry Jackson, R. C. Jebb and F. W. Maitland, Henry Sidgwick and J. N. Keynes, C. S. Kenny, J. J. Thompson, and A. W. Verrall, and the brothers George and Francis Darwin.

But some considerable figures, among them Alfred Marshall, Lowes Dickinson, McTaggart the philosopher and Leonard Whibley were in the opposition ranks. Yet it seems that rejection was in the main backed by men not resident in Cambridge. The story goes that on the day of the vote a platform at Liverpool Street was notably crowded with clergy who declared that they were going, as geographically as they could do on the Great Eastern Railway, 'to *Bury* St Edmund's'. They may not all have known that their funerary wrath was being directed not against the saint once buried in the great Suffolk abbey, but against a thirteenth-century Archbishop of Canterbury. In the upshot the application was non-placeted, and the little foundation carried on as a lodging place for Catholic ordinands who were reading for Cambridge degrees. No laymen, by now, were allowed to reside there.

The 'seminary' period of St Edmund's existence continued for another ten years. But as the English hierarchy gave up the idea of sending ordinands to the University very few church students ever came there. But it was found that St Edmund's could provide a somewhat segregated place of residence in Cambridge for men who were already priests and who wished to read for degrees.

The first extension of the buildings came in 1917 and included a Perpendicular Gothic chapel by the priest-architect Fr Benedict Williamson, who had already designed the Franciscans' church at Oxford. A peak period was reached in the late 1930s and afterwards, and more buildings, among them the lower part of the block which contains the hall, were then put up.

An important mastership at this period was that of Fr John Petit, till recently the Bishop of the Roman Catholic diocese of Menevia, which includes most of Wales. As St Edmund's was still unrecognised by the University arrangements were at first made for its residents to be accepted by the Non-Collegiate Students Board. Later on, most St Edmund's men became members either of Christ's or Downing. In the post-war years a few laymen came to St Edmund's, but till the crucial year of 1945 most of those who found their way there were already priests.

The modern period in this history of St Edmund's was ushered in by the epoch-making Bridges report of 1962. As a result of that report, recognition was sought as an approved, post-graduate society within the University. It was granted in 1965, and from then onwards there were great changes in a foundation now included within the University's collegiate system.

St Edmund's still provides living accommodation for priests who are reading for first degrees and must belong to other colleges. But this side of its work has diminished, and there seems to be no likelihood of its expansion.

The Master must still be a Catholic priest, but the Fellows, though they must be committed to Christian ideals, need not be of the Roman allegiance. Neither they nor the post-graduates, coming from several countries and with a wide range of higher studies, need be clergy, and though about a quarter of St Edmund's research and post-graduate members are in Orders, the proportion of laity, and of non-Catholics, is far higher than it was in 1965. Yet the College stands firmly within the Christian tradition, offering a 'serenity of mind proper to those who have the security of faith'; the pattern of its life and work may, perhaps, be taken as that of an ideal or typical Christian college.

Uniquely in Cambridge, the domestic arrangements of St Edmund's are in the hands of a small group of Sisters, with their own little convent at one end of the buildings as so far extended.

St Edmund's plans for expansion will mean a further increase in its buildings, along with changes in those which now exist. Plans for new buildings, both communal and residential have been got out by Mr Douglas Harding, of the Cambridge architects Lyster, Grillet and Harding. They allow for the vital element of a larger hall, for junior and senior combination rooms, for a new library, a conference room, and some seminar rooms. Single and married sets are also due to be provided. Though tenders for the first of these buildings had been received by the early days of 1973, no building work had been started by the end of January.

Though St Edmund's will always look, for its main support, to the Roman Catholic Church, it intends, as the ecumenical movement develops, to seek a broader basis. It thus has, and will have, the chance to produce outstanding work by cross fertilisation of worldwide Roman Catholic scholarship and the historic tradition of our older Universities as these have themselves developed during seven centuries.

CLARE HALL

At the end of the section on Clare College I mentioned the scheme, put forward by Clare and sanctioned in 1966, for an 'Approved Foundation' which would give a collegiate home to some of the more senior post-graduates who are now in Cambridge on various teaching and research work. With the help of two American organisations a daughter College, originated by Clare but now a wholly separate foundation, has now had some years of corporate existence. Clare Hall, as it is fittingly called, has seen its new buildings completed, and can look back on some five years of a pioneering social career.

As Darwin College was founded by the combined initiative of Caius, St John's, and Trinity, so the new graduate College in Herschel Road is Clare's particular effort to help solve the great problem caused by the vast (and in the opinion of some University members excessive) influx of research and other post-graduate workers who have lately come to work in Cambridge. Many of these men and women are senior people, of long experience and in some cases of great eminence, who cannot get fellowships in the older colleges but who are doing important teaching in the University or who are on what are called 'borderline' aspects of supervision and higher research. Many of them are married and have families.

Although by 1964, when Clare Hall's inception was agreed in the parent college, the idea had taken root in Cambridge that such colleges as Churchill should within their college boundaries provide married quarters for some post-graduate members, no new college had yet allowed for the full residential integration, in the heart of its main buildings, of such visitors with their wives and children.

It was a college of this closely knit type, which duly became an approved foundation within the University, and whose buildings are now complete with their novel in-college element of the wives and children of some of the male residents, that Clare brought into being.

Like some other recent foundations in Cambridge, Clare Hall had a corporate existence before possessing buildings of its own. What came first was the formal establishment, in February of 1966, of Clare Hall as an approved foundation, and the working out of financial arrangements whereby the money made available by Clare College was augmented by lesser, but handsome American gifts from the Ford Foundation and the Old Dominion Trust. The new college's funds were, and are, administered by the parent college, acting as the trustee of Clare Hall. The income is handed, for spending at its own discretion, to Clare Hall.

Back in 1964, a provisional council was set up, initially manned by the Master and six Fellows of Clare, but soon enlarged from outside. Early in 1966 this governing body handed the new foundation to the first President, Dr A. B. Pippard, of Clare, and the first of the full Fellows whose activities in Cambridge were to be helped by the money now available. Those Fellows soon increased, so that several men and women benefited from the Clare Hall scheme who could not use the ancient College's existing buildings. The social life, particularly lunches and dinners, which is of the essence of a College was, however, modestly kept up. The small dining hall and the Master's dining room in Clare were available for a time, while during two academic years, from 1967 to 1969, regular dinners were held in the newly built University Centre.

From the autumn of 1966, building work was in progress on the Herschel Road site which had been obtained from St John's, and early in 1967 the fair-sized house of 'Elmside', at the eastern end of the site, became available for residential use on the death of its occupant, Dr Berry of Downing. It was fitted out, and is still used, to accommodate some unmarried visiting Fellows and post-graduate students; its fine garden is an attractive feature between the older house and Clare Hall's new group of buildings.

Once corporate life had started, the next important step was to put up buildings which would provide dining and entertaining room for all Clare Hall's members, and living quarters, single or married, for those who wish, during their stay in Cambridge, to live in college. A precedent for Cambridge was set when the architect was chosen. For although Mr Ralph Erskine is British by birth, he practices in Sweden and works within the modern Scandinavian tradition.

The new buildings were finished in time for the autumn term of 1969, and they were opened by Sir Eric Ashby, Master of Clare, on the last day of his Vice-Chancellorship. Their completion, and the start of their use by a social and residential community, marked an important phase in the history of Clare Hall.

As an academic society, Clare Hall, with Fellows (some of them holding teaching posts in the University) visiting Fellows, research Fellows, graduate research students, and associates, has now existed for nearly seven years. Extra funds have come in from the Old Dominion Trust.

The visiting Fellows, a class comparatively new to Cambridge, have mostly come from overseas; some have found their stay in Cambridge a convenient staging point before a move to other work in this country or elsewhere. Scholars from the United States have made up the largest group among them, but many other countries, in Europe and elsewhere, have been represented.

The younger post-graduates, first arriving in the autumn of 1967, are more numerous now than at first; whether they become about half of Clare Hall's membership must partly depend on how far post-graduate research is to expand in the University. The associates, like the visiting Fellows in that they have come to work in Cambridge but belong to no other college, are members of Clare Hall but without the Fellows' right to have some of their meals at the college's expense.

An important proof of Clare Hall's success must come from the experience, longer than one whole year can give, of the residential arrangement which has brought complete families to live in close company in an academic complex. Professor Pippard and his family now live in Clare Hall, and children are found in the families who now inhabit some of Mr Erskine's new buildings. Some residents, in addition to those in 'Elmside', are unmarried; and the total membership of the College is nearly 140.

The buildings of Clare Hall are the first in Cambridge designed by an architect from Scandinavia; as such they can be seen as a smaller, more humane opposite number to Arne Jacobsen's St Catherine's at Oxford. Some of the furniture comes from Scandinavia, and some pieces were designed by Mr Erskine. The buildings themselves have some Scandinavian touches, notably the long expanses of sloping roof and the conspicuous, over capacious, and somewhat unattractive water chutes which are frequently in evidence.

The layout is ingeniously divided between the living quarters on each side of 'Family Walk', and the working, administrative, and social part of the college. On this eastern side of the building one finds a reading room and a meeting room, while members can rent quiet studies away from domestic turmoil. Children, moreover, may not enter what is known as 'Scholars' Walk'.

Not far from the offices, the pleasantly furnished sitting room is what more traditional colleges would call a senior common room, and in the dining room (alias hall) there is no high table. Wives are freely admitted to dine here along with their husbands, and children are not barred from coming in to lunch, provided that they remember that a lunch in Cambridge can be a time for talking business rather than for social pleasantries, so that tact and common sense are needed among these junior inhabitants of Clare Hall. Better seen than heard is, one presumes, a ruling maxim.

As a French chef has been installed in the kitchen, Clare Hall has quickly built up an excellent reputation for the fare provided. This gastronomic point may well explain the fact that this colony of a college whose history goes back well over six hundred years has so far made a good start with the social arrangements which, for some of its members (and for all of them as and when they come in to meals), are very remote from anything which could have figured in the thinking of Richard de Badew and Lady Clare.

HUGHES HALL

THE College, for the teacher training of women graduates, which is now known as Hughes Hall, has been in the University since 1949 when it gained the status of a recognised institution. More recently, in 1969, its status was elevated to that of an Approved Society. Its original inclusion within the official fold of Cambridge University may be seen as part of the same move which, in 1948, gave full University status to members of Girton and Newnham. But like Girton and Newnham it had started, in the Victorian period, outside the University although, like Newnham (its academic godmother and original neighbour) within the town of Cambridge. Many of those who actively encouraged the University education of women were behind this move for the provision, within easy reach of the facilities and lecturers of Cambridge, of teacher training better than that which most women could in those days obtain.

The idea that a College should be started for this purpose in Cambridge had gained ground by the opening months of 1885, the first discussions on the matter being held in Miss Clough's rooms at Newnham. A committee was formed, and among its members were Oscar Browning (in a few more years to become Principal of Cambridge University Day Training College), the Rev. G. Forrest Browne of St Catharine's who later became Bishop of Bristol, Mrs Hort, Miss Buss the well-known Principal of the North London Collegiate School, and its secretary Mrs Verrall who was the wife of A. W. Verrall of Trinity, the brilliant and in some ways controversial Greek scholar of that time. Professor Liveing of St John's, Mrs Peile and others soon joined the committee.

A memorandum produced by the committee explained that, apart from the opportunities for teacher training which existed in London and Cheltenham it was necessary that more facilities should be created for 'the more technical part' of women's teacher training, and that it was advisable for this to be done in Cambridge. The main purpose of any new foundation would be the training of 'educated' women who intended to teach. No woman under eighteen should enter, and those who came should have obtained good qualifications. The committee further explained that a 'very competent' principal had been found, and that a house for her and eight students had been earmarked for the new foundation.

Enough support was gained for the College to be opened, in a house at Newnham, for the autumn term of 1885. Its title, in those early days and for some years to come, was The Cambridge Training College for Women Teachers. The first Principal, from whom the College later took its name, was Miss E. P. Hughes, a Welsh lady who had been one of Miss Beale's pupils at Cheltenham Ladies' College, and who gained some years' teaching experience at Cheltenham and elsewhere until, in 1881, she went up to Newnham. There, in 1884, she got a first in the Moral Sciences Tripos, and she read history in her last year. Her original students at Cambridge numbered fourteen; several others failed, through lack of accommodation, to gain places in the little College.

A project for a 'collegiate' building, to hold 25 trainees, was soon considered, and in 1886 an appeal for some £7,000 was launched. Among many headmistresses of endowed or proprietary girls' schools who backed the idea were the heads of Clifton and Redland High Schools in Bristol and those far-famed educational spinsters Miss Buss and Miss Beale. Another house in Newnham was soon taken over, and before the permanent new buildings could be started the College, soon popular and well filled, moved in 1888 to the part of Cambridge which now contains it. Quarters were taken up in a house in Queen Anne Terrace overlooking Parker's Piece. Another house in the same terrace was soon rented and, in 1892 when many more students were in residence, five more houses, not far away from the College, had been brought into use.

Soon after 1890 Professor Liveing became Chairman of the College Council. A little later, Roman Catholic students were admitted, at a time when very few Catholics came up to the University itself. Their new church of Our Lady and the English Martyrs was conveniently near, and they did their teaching practice in Cambridge's two Roman Catholic schools. The College soon gained a reputation for originality in its training methods. Its students went out, for practice, to numerous schools in the town, and in 1893 two of the College's one-time students were in charge of the Perse Preparatory School.

The time now came to start new and more spacious buildings, and to overcome the inconvenience to the College of being dispersed in as many as seven houses. Of the money needed for a new building, £3,000 came from the will of Newnham's important benefactress, Miss Emily Pfeiffer. A site in Wollaston Road was obtained from Caius College and in 1893 W. M. Fawcett, who had also designed the new building for the Perse School not far away, was appointed as the Training College's architect. Flemish Renaissance or Jacobean in style, with its second-floor windows capped by little gables alternately rounded or triangular, the new building was L-shaped with a meeting room and a dining room in the lower limb of the L. Its main gables, in deep red terracotta, are very Dutch in style, while the initials C.W.T.C. and the key dates of 1885 and 1895 still decorate its porch. A fine feature of the site is the excellent view of Fenner's which the College's occupants can enjoy from its upper windows.

The intense activity of the 1890s seems to have put a strain on Miss Hughes' health, for in 1898 she was given an assistant and in 1899 resigned for reasons of health. Fifty years later, when it became a part of the University, the College was fittingly named after her. She later did important educational work in Japan, Wales, and elsewhere, and died in 1925.

Miss Hughes' two successors at the Training College had short spells of office. Then there followed, from 1908 to 1933, the long, consolidating régime of Miss M. H. Wood. By the time that she left, the College's students averaged between 40 and 50, and rose to about 60 by the time that the Second World War broke out. The two adjacent houses had by then been rented from Caius, while in 1937 an extension to the original block was finished, in a simple neo-Georgian style and by a London architect, Mr Verner Rees, who later designed several buildings for the University of Birmingham.

An immediate post-war landmark in the College's history was its inclusion in the University. Its student numbers have now risen to just over 90, all of them post-graduates and one of them (in 1970) researching for a doctorate. About a third of Hughes Hall's members are out in lodgings, while a few come from overseas. Should the College's membership continue to rise, space is available on the long, somewhat narrow site, for a single-storey block of extra buildings. In the meantime Hughes Hall continues steadily within its originally appointed task of training women, with good academic records, for the teaching profession.

The College's work is done in close association with the University's Department of Education, and some of its seminar and lecture rooms are used by that Department. Hughes Hall's students take the Department of Education's course and, as education itself has widened out to include new subjects, so the subjects read at Hughes Hall have inevitably increased. Both academically and in the domestic sense, it is a far cry from the original arrangements of nearly ninety years ago.

SELECT BIBLIOGRAPHY

THE literature of Cambridge is far too vast for all authorities to be listed here. I have therefore concentrated on works which, apart from material on the city and the University in general, have something on each College which existed at the time when they came out. I have also listed a good many of the books which are available on individual Colleges. I realise, of course, that there is, as yet, little to hand on the most recent foundations. Some of the works which I list have a mainly historical approach; others deal primarily with architecture and its associated arts.

R. Willis and J. W. Clark's *The Architectural History of the University of Cambridge*, 4 *vols*, 1886, remains an indispensable classic both for history and architecture; it is well supplemented, in a shorter work, by T. D. Atkinson and J. W. Clark's *Cambridge Described and Illustrated*, 1897. Later works of interest and importance include M. A. R. Tuker, *Cambridge*, 1907, Arthur Gray, Cambridge University, 1926, and B. W. Downs, *Cambridge Past and Present*, 1926. More recent works include Nikolaus Pevsnér, *Cambridgeshire* (Buildings of England series), 1954, Bryan Little and A. F. Kersting, *Portrait of Cambridge*, 3rd impression, 1957, and Bryan Little, *Cambridge Discovered*, 1960. Of immense importance are Vol III (1959) of the Victoria County History of Cambridgeshire and the Isle of Ely, and the two volumes on the City of Cambridge, issued in 1959 by the Royal Commission on Historic Monuments. Nicholas Taylor and others *Cambridge New Architecture* (3rd edn, 1972) is important for modern buildings.

Coming to individual College histories, vital details can still be gleaned from the volumes in the 'light blue' series brought out, shortly before and soon after 1900, by the now defunct London publishers F. E. Robinson and

Co; they also produced a similar series on the Colleges at Oxford. For a few Colleges, despite the passing of some seven decades, no volumes have yet appeared to continue their story. I can only hope that three Colleges at least will, in the 1980s when they keep centenaries, do something to remedy their particular defects. The 'light blue' list is as follows: Peterhouse, T. A. Walker, 1906. Clare, J. A. Wardale, 1899. Gonville and Caius, John Venn, 1901, reprinted 1923 and 1935. Trinity Hall, H. E. Malden, 1902. Corpus Christi, H. P. Stokes, 1898. King's, A. Austen Leigh, 1899. Queens', J. H. Gray, 1899, and 1926. St Catharine's, G. Forrest Browne, 1902. Jesus, Arthur Gray, 1902 (second and augmented edn, F. Brittain, 1960). Christ's, John Peile, 1900. St John's, J. B. Mullinger, 1901. Magdalene, E. K. Purnell, 1904. Emmanuel, E. S. Shuckburgh, 1904. Sidney Sussex, G. Maclean Edwards, 1899. Downing, H. W. P. Stevens, 1899. Selwyn, A. L. Brown, 1906.

For the first two women's Colleges one has M. C. Bradbrook *That Infidel Place* (Girton), 1969, and Mary Agnes Hamilton, *Newnham*, 1936.

For some of the men's Colleges one has, in addition to short guides and booklets, more recent works of greater substance. Among them are: King's Hall, A. B. Cobban, 1969. Clare, *Clare College*, 1326–1926, 2 vols, 1928, 1930. Pembroke, Aubrey Attwater, 1936. Corpus Christi (for the period 1822–1952) J. P. T. Bury, 1952. Queens', C. T. Seltman, 1951. St Catharine's, W. H. S. Jones, 1951. Christ's (early history) A. H. Lloyd, 1934. St John's, Edward Miller, 1961. Trinity, G. M. Trevelyan, 1943. Sidney Sussex, C. W. Scott Giles, 1951.

INDEX